Praise for C

"Since Luther, Christians have understood that all believers are called to vocations to serve God and humanity in whatever capacity they find themselves. But Christopher Richmann identifies danger signs in current language about calling to the ordained ministry, especially the concept of an 'inner calling,' which he sees as posing a potential threat to the general Christian calling to vocation. In this thoughtful book Richmann raises very important questions and suggests fruitful ways forward to strengthening the vocations of all Christians."

—**MARK GRANQUIST**, Lloyd and Annelotte Svendsbye Professor of the History of Christianity, Luther Seminary, St. Paul, Minnesota

"Richmann challenges the emphasis on an 'inner call' to the office of ministry by centering the ministerial call within the broader parameters of Luther's understanding of vocation: vocation as service that benefits our neighbors, and God's call encountered in our present circumstances rather than beckoning us from the future. He moves back and forth between discussing historical Lutheran views and offering his own personal and pastoral experiences."

—**KATHRYN KLEINHANS**, dean, Trinity Lutheran Seminary at Capital University, Columbus, Ohio

CALLED

CALLED

RECOVERING LUTHERAN PRINCIPLES FOR MINISTRY AND VOCATION

CHRISTOPHER J. RICHMANN

Fortress Press
Minneapolis

CALLED
Recovering Lutheran Principles for Ministry and Vocation

Cover image: Cloth on baptismal font, IStock Photos / BuckleyPics
Cover Design: Lindsey Owens

Print ISBN: 978-1-5064-8130-2
eBook ISBN: 978-1-5064-8131-9

Contents

Contents

Abbreviations

ALC	American Lutheran Church
BC	*The Book of Concord*, ed. Robert Kolb and Timothy J. Wengert (Minneapolis: Fortress, 2000).
ELC	Evangelical Lutheran Church
ELCA	Evangelical Lutheran Church in America
ILCW	Inter-Lutheran Commission on Worship
LCA	Lutheran Church in America
LCMS	Lutheran Church–Missouri Synod
LW	*Luther's Works*, ed. Jaroslav Pelikan and Helmut T. Lehmann, American ed., 55 vols. (Philadelphia: Fortress; St. Louis: Concordia, 1955–86).
ULCA	United Lutheran Church in America
WA	*Luthers Werke: Kritische Gesamtausgabe* (Schriften), 73 vols. (Weimar, Germany: H. Böhlau, 1883–2009).

Abbreviations

INTRODUCTION

THE PROCESS OF ENTRY into ordained (or "commissioned" or "rostered") ministry looks different in different denominations. Within denominations, this process can vary depending on the priorities of the church leadership or decision-making body overseeing the approval of candidates into ministry. In those Christian fellowships where the governance structures are more congregation centered, this process can look drastically different from one person's experience to another's. So what I'm about to relate here should not be taken as representative, but I have good reason to believe the circumstances are not unique.

After completing a master's degree at a Lutheran seminary, I began a PhD program in church history and simultaneously began serving a rural Texas congregation of the Evangelical Lutheran Church in America (ELCA) as a "synodically authorized worship leader"—my synod's somewhat awkward category for persons approved for the ministry of word and sacrament in an ad hoc capacity within a specific setting but not "ordained" to ministry in the sense of bearing approval to serve the church at large or enter the official, centralized placement process for ministry at other sites within the denomination. I very much enjoyed my ministry. And although I occasionally had to explain to congregants that I was not ordained (usually when someone asked me to officiate a wedding), for the most part, this in-between status did not inhibit my ministry. I was their pastor. I heard their confessions and pronounced their forgiveness. I led their worship. I taught Bible studies. I administered Holy Communion to them. I baptized their children and grandchildren, confirmed the youth, and buried their parents, spouses, and children. I prayed with them at the bedside and visited them in the hospital. I even parked in the "clergy parking" when I made those hospital visits. As far as the church members were concerned, I was their pastor. It was my denomination and the IRS that labeled it differently.

Due to life circumstances, I began to consider the process of moving from a synodically authorized worship leader to a rostered minister. At that point, I had served the congregation for seven years. I did the research and sought guidance from leaders and fellow ministers. I was prepared for the possibility of needing to demonstrate my fitness: a proper ministry internship, clinical pastoral education, coursework in pastoral care or preaching, demonstration of competency in biblical languages. What I was not prepared for was the first question directed at me in my first candidacy interview. A lay member of the candidacy committee put the question succinctly: "Can you describe for us your sense of your inner call to ministry?"

As soon as I heard the question, I recalled having seen this term, *inner call*, in some of the preparation materials I had received. But I had not given it much thought, mostly because I was naively certain it was not a very important issue. Although I had not yet theologically or historically analyzed the concept in any depth, "inner call" seemed to me to be an unnecessary category—both practically and in terms of the theological tradition of my Lutheran denomination. The Augsburg Confession—the central Lutheran statement of faith—makes no mention of an "inner call," saying only in article 14 that "no one should publicly teach, preach, or administer the sacraments without a proper call."[1] That much I knew from my Lutheran confessions course in seminary, and we never talked about an "inner call" in that class. More than that, "inner call" seemed to me to taste of a certain kind of "enthusiasm"—that is, a belief that God reveals himself inwardly (in the soul, the mind, the affections) instead of or beyond external revelation in word and sacrament. Having come back to Lutheranism after nearly a decade in Pentecostal and charismatic circles ("back" because I was raised in the Lutheran Church—Missouri Synod), I was sensitive to what I considered to be the dangers of counting on God to reveal himself inwardly: I was never sure if the voice I heard was God's, mine, or some echo of the voices in the world around me. To me, this was the genius and great comfort of Lutheranism—God speaks quite plainly through created things, not cryptically in one's inner recesses.

Sitting on an uncomfortable chair in a conference room of our synod headquarters and feeling my heart rate increase, I attempted to reply to the committee member's question without either disrespecting the earnest query or accepting its premises.

"I don't really think of my journey toward candidacy for ministry in terms of an 'inner call,'" I said. "I believe that I have gifts to offer the church, the church has needs, and I am willing to serve. I'm not sure there is anything necessary beyond that."

I could tell immediately that my answer was not satisfactory. Part of the problem, they explained, was that I had not indicated clearly in my application materials whether I wanted to pursue becoming an ordained minister (word and sacrament) or an associate in ministry (some combination of word and service). I told them I wasn't really sure, but I was hoping that the candidacy committee could make recommendations to me based on my qualifications and other contextual information.

I was politely told to try again. The candidacy committee asked me to spend a few months in further "discernment" about my call and consider how I might articulate my sense of an inner call to ministry. After conferring with a pastor friend, I returned to the candidacy committee speaking unambiguously about my desire to seek *ordained* ministry, and I intentionally used words like "joy," "commitment," and "feeling compelled" when asked further about my sense of an inner call. In other words, I deliberately emphasized the personal, subjective experience in my ministry and preparation for ministry. But I continued to voice a concern about the appropriateness of the concept.

By God's grace, the committee was satisfied that I had articulated an inner call, perhaps in spite of myself. "Senses his personal call" was how they put it in my entrance letter. A year later, I was ordained and called to serve as a pastor by the same congregation I had served by that time for eight years.

I describe this experience at length because it is the genesis of this book. I wanted to understand how the concept of an inner call to ministry gained such a prominent role in Lutheran thought and practice even though it does not appear in our confessions. Today, Lutherans commonly speak of an "inner call" to ministry. In 1986, one scholar discovered that "the concept of the 'secret call' is alive and well among some Lutheran pre-ministerial and ministerial students, and among some of its clergy."[2] The concept has only gained ground: the ELCA, the largest American Lutheran denomination, now regards the inner call as necessary.

I also wanted to uncover if and how this concept fits into the bedrock convictions of Lutherans; after all, an absence of the term or concept in the confessions doesn't necessarily mean it is at odds with them. But this quest quickly became about more than truing Lutheran practice to Lutheran theology. In my further study of vocation, I came to recognize a concept that had the potential to offer a word to the wider church about service, duty, and evangelization that was at once sobering and liberating.

Having discovered in the Lutheran heritage principles for ministerial call that say something different and needed for today's church, I sought an explanation for why these principles do not play a larger role in how people offer themselves and receive authorization for public ministry. This is a historical question. The first part of this book is a historical investigation, traced through prominent thought leaders, into the inner call concept in American Lutheranism, from its European foundations, through its American development, up to the present day.

This is the first time such research has appeared in print, which might suggest it deserves more exhaustive treatment than I present here.[3] That is probably true. But it's not my intent to pursue subtle academic questions. Rather, I aim to tell a story that helps explain why Lutherans have not led from their own principles or been able to offer their distinct voice to the wider discussion about ministerial call.

This topic deserves critical investigation, since *how* one is called to ministry touches both practice and theology. The lack of scholarship contributes to a state of confusion in today's Lutheran discourse—some consider the inner call so natural that they assume it has always been a normal or even required part of the Lutheran call process,[4] while others consider it so foreign that they assume Lutherans have rarely taught it.[5] Both are incorrect. Martin Luther had only criticism for the inner call as he encountered it in the "enthusiasts"—that is, as an experience devoid of any irrefutable external divine confirmation—and as already mentioned, the concept is absent from the Lutheran confessions. Beginning, however, with scholastic Lutheran theologians (often called "orthodox") in the seventeenth century, Lutherans have a rich, unbroken history of entertaining, embracing, developing, and systematizing the notion of an inner call. Throughout these developments, many definitions for *inner call* appeared, most being some combination of qualifications and sensing a divinely placed desire for the ministry. As I hope will become clear in the pages that follow, any description of a "call" to ministry that is not wholly identified as the explicit or implicit request of a neighbor is an "inner call" in some form, whether that term appears or not.

Beyond showing that the inner call has a large—but not original— role in Lutheranism, this historical account should demonstrate that the inner call fits uneasily into the Lutheran system of thought. Clear correlations between the theology of the sacraments (the Lord's Supper, baptism, and proclamation) and the doctrine of ministerial call among major sixteenth-century reformers suggest that this was not a side issue but was intimately woven into how early Protestants viewed God's activity in the world. Luther's full confidence in the physical elements of the sacraments to confer God's grace reverberated in his belief that the external call to ministry through other humans was sufficient to make a minister. Conversely, the suspicion of Luther's former Wittenberg colleague Andreas Karlstadt and the influential non-Lutheran reformer John Calvin that material elements are not able to convey divinity in the sacraments correlated with their beliefs that an external call was not sufficient and some nonmaterial, spiritual "inner" call was necessary. Although embracing the inner call does not necessarily imperil traditional Lutheran sacramental teaching, this correlation has reappeared, most notably in the "American Lutheranism" of the nineteenth century following the great Lutheran organizer and first widely influential American Lutheran theologian Samuel Simon Schmucker.

More directly, the inner call teaching also in many cases distorted the original Lutheran vision regarding ministerial call. In the generations after Luther, early orthodox and Pietist leaders simply accepted that some might have an inner call experience, seeing it as a possible addition to the external call (from church bodies, congregations, etc.), which up to that point Lutherans had equated with the "proper call" (or "regular call") of the Augsburg Confession. Later orthodox writers touted the necessity of the inner call but remained vague about its relation to the external call. In the nineteenth century, American Lutherans began to argue that the inner call was *part* of the "regular call" of the Augsburg Confession. From there, it was a seemingly smooth development for some to argue that the external call was *dependent* on the inner call and only served to ratify the inner call. In other words, the external call did not make the minister, as Luther argued; the inner call did. The external call—while still necessary—was demoted to the status of "from humans," while the inner call was "from God." These views have not been mere matters of private conviction or isolated to one area of the church's organizational mechanics. As my own experience shows, when the external call is made dependent on the inner call, the inner call has functionally become the ruler of the process.

The second part of this book attempts to reestablish ministerial call upon classic Lutheran commitments. To illustrate the importance of this issue for the life of the church today, I sprinkle these theological chapters with personal observations and conversations with pastors and nonordained believers.

Martin Luther was not a systematic theologian in terms of writing highly structured, exhaustive, and abstract theology. His work, like Saint Paul's, arose out of the immediate needs of the church. Yet Luther's theology shows a remarkable consistency and cohesion so that one can easily make connections between principles and specific arguments. Perhaps the most ill-fitting aspect of the inner call teaching among Lutherans is that it weakens the connection between the Lutheran principle of vocation and the specific teaching on ministerial vocation. Among those who embraced the inner call, a doctrine of ministerial call developed that put the Lutheran teaching on vocation in the periphery.

The Lutheran perspective of vocation centers on attending to the requests and needs one encounters in the material world. In most cases, we know we are called to some task because we literally hear someone make a request of us. The fact that we may hear more calls than we can attend to or that we may hear potentially conflicting calls only means that God graciously offers us myriad opportunities to serve. The gospel frees us from worrying whether there is a single, perfect, or completely sinless option when we decide whom to respond to and how. Often these callings are very explicit. A boss asks an employee to finish a report by the end of the week. A woman asks her neighbor to watch her child for an hour so she can run errands. A wife asks her husband to pick up dinner on the way home from work. Even inarticulate calls are easily understood. The crying newborn asks his mother to feed him. Sometimes the call is implied rather than stated outright. Children sitting at their desks, facing a teacher at the start of a school day, are calling the one adult in the room to teach. The wife's expectation that her husband will love and serve her is a call to the husband to bring home dinner without always being asked. Many of these callings (both explicit and implicit) are associated with what we call "vocations," in the sense of some commonly understood distinct office or relationship: one's role as a father, student, physician, and so on. We preserve the spirit of this when we speak of doctors being "on call." But many are also occasional (and these are more often explicit), arising in the apparently chance encounters of life and not essentially related to one's vocation. This distinction between occasional callings and vocations is often ignored, although it is crucial. A man may answer a call to help change his neighbor's car tire, but others are employed, licensed car mechanics. The world needs both.

As an occasional calling *and* a vocation (office), gospel ministry is special in that it alone deals with the words of eternal life. But this does not mean it rests on a special kind of call. Its difference comes from its *effects*. Through all other vocations, God maintains the old world; only through the gospel ministry does God create the new world. While this does not rule out the possibility of a divine inner call (God can do what God wants), it means we should be wary of enthroning the inner call as a norm or expectation. God calls people to ministry in the same way God calls all people to all other vocations—through the needy requests of the material world. In recognizing ministerial call, Luther would have us look at two things: people who call a minister and a minister who serves out of love and duty. Commentators often imply that Luther's negative views on the inner call don't apply because his situation was so different from ours today: Luther was criticizing those who, on the basis of an inner call, thought they needed *no external call*, and this is not likely to be the case facing our churches today. But that is to miss Luther's fundamental insight: an inner call is not necessary when creation calls and a person responds in love and duty—this is already a closed circuit. Beyond this, inner call theology runs afoul of two key Lutheran principles: it reinforces a world-denying spirituality rooted in monasticism, and it applies Scripture selectively and without regard for the law-gospel perspective.

Some are called in an official, ongoing manner. In this case, those who call the minister give a public and often written request for this person's ministry, and this call applies implicitly to that person's ongoing relationships with the congregants and their spheres of living. This person is commonly known as a "called and ordained" minister. This ministry is not beholden to people's unscriptural demands but shaped definitively by the gospel itself and includes equipping the saints themselves for ministry. And this call—much like the expectations between spouses—doesn't need to be constantly reiterated. The congregation members don't need to formally request for their minister to preach every Sunday. Of course, this call also means that this person is likely to receive a more-than-average number of explicit and personal requests to minister—this is the person people call on the telephone (or text, as is increasingly the case these days) to baptize their children, officiate at a funeral, and visit and pray with the sick. Reorienting ministerial call to the concrete requests of neighbors and loving duty to respond is a simple yet profound answer to some of the most worrisome features of the professional ministry today: lack of vocational certainty and commitment.

This shamelessly earthy view of a call can help Christians make good on a central promise of Protestant thought: the universal priesthood of believers. Every believer who has ears (or other senses) to perceive the call of the neighbor is called to minister. These calls come implicitly and explicitly, and where responding to these calls does not cause offense or disrupt the good order of the church, the one called is commanded by God to minister. Christians have not been good at this ministry partly because of a vaunted view of the ministerial calling (of which an "inner call" is one factor) and partly because they have not been trained to hear the creature waiting (as Luther said) or to speak the words of life. Going back especially to the orthodox theologians, Christians have been classified as "preachers" and "hearers"—a misleading distinction that robs the world of gospel proclamation and leads Christians to unnecessarily spiritualize their earthly callings for want

of a sense of divine vocation. Instead, the church should teach believers their duty and equip them to proclaim and teach God's word to one
another, especially within family relationships. This involves a reorienting also of what it is that gospel ministers proclaim. Christians who
are not public ministers tend to be reluctant to preach because they
think part of what they are to proclaim is either the academic and intel-
lectual material covered in seminary or their own inspiring experience
of grace. Lacking either of these, they feel unequipped. In reality, the
message is so simple and straightforward that the least educated and
the most sinful rascal can proclaim it. The church is a creature of the
word. Perhaps a manifold increase in the proclamation of God's church-
creating word is just what is needed in this era of church "decline."

Another neglected aspect of the common priesthood is the right
and duty to judge teaching. No single subset of the church—for instance,
clergy, bishops, or seminary faculty—can be the sole securer of correct
doctrine. Neither can any subset of the church be excluded from this
work. The same vocational concern for our neighbors that leads directly
to ministry also drives the indirect work of guarding and promoting
pure gospel proclamation. We are obligated, not just for the sake of our
own salvation but for the salvation of those God has put in our lives, to
ensure someone fills the office of ministry, judge what we hear from our
public ministers, and support public ministers in their work of word and
sacrament.

This book is written for the church—the *whole* church. I hope to
make good on this claim in three ways. First, it is a challenge for all
those concerned with calling ministers to carefully consider their own
roles and the assumptions and practices involved. This means congregations that encourage people to consider preparing for the ministry
and vote to call ministers; pastors who model the ministerial calling;
denominational leadership that sets rhetoric, protocol, and policy; college and seminary personnel who help potential ministers think theologically about the call; candidacy committees that serve as gatekeepers
to the office of ministry; and, of course, potential ministers themselves.

In short, all believers have a stake in how their ministers are called and how their ministers *think* about their calling.

Second, I hope to remind readers that the gospel ministry does not belong exclusively to those who are ordained. The whole church has the duty and joy of proclaiming what God wants to say to a lost and dying world. As Lutherans have taught for five centuries, the "keys of the kingdom of heaven" (Matt 16:19) are not connected in some essential way to any training, preparation, ceremony, office, or type of person. Rather, Jesus distributes the keys upon hearing the confession of his Christhood (Matt 16:13–19). This would be reason enough to recite the Apostles' Creed every Sunday: it not only reminds us of what binds us together as believers, but it naturally leads to our commissioning as God's heavenly key turners.

Finally, this book is also written for the whole church in the sense of offering a biblical vision of God's evangelical activity in the world. While it finds inspiration from Lutheran theology and primarily analyzes the Lutheran tradition, it is ecumenically hopeful. Building on a scriptural view of creation, it offers a clarity and simplicity about ministerial call that can combat anxiety and doubt and counter the needless time and energy so many invest in their process of vocational "discernment." Provided the church employs other moral and theological safeguards to avoid scandal or error, it can only benefit from having proclaimers assured of their call and reassured with each new request from their neighbors.

1 EUROPEAN FOUNDATIONS

REFORMATION ERA

CHRISTIAN THEOLOGY AND PRACTICE burst open in the sixteenth century. Within a few years of Martin Luther's *Ninety-Five Theses* in 1517, nearly every aspect of Christianity—from the Bible, to the sacraments, to the church—had come under scrutiny. For all the major Protestant leaders, freedom from Catholic dogma meant room to see one's central assumptions to their logical conclusions—including their views on how God calls people to the office of ministry.

A survey of the theology of ministerial call among key Protestant reformers reveals the range of thinking on this issue. Studied in relation to each leader's teaching on the sacraments, such a survey also shows how the distinct commitments of each thinker come out in the teaching on ministerial call. To get a rounded picture and provide crucial points of reference for later discussions in this book, we need to look not only at Luther and the Lutheran confessions but at an early supporter of Luther who became his adversary and a monumentally influential non-Lutheran who attempted throughout his career to find common ground with Lutherans.

MARTIN LUTHER

After 1517, Martin Luther increasingly recognized that his contro-versy with the dominant Catholic theology was not simply a matter of indulgences or abuses. The fault line ran deeper, penetrating to the core human concern: Where do humans meet God? When Luther accused his opponents of works righteousness, he was naming their theological assumption that salvation was the culmination of human attempts to ascend to God through the performance of works (assisted by varying amounts of grace) that supposedly conformed one to God's image or will. Instead, for Luther, "the gospel is good news because it is the proclamation that fellowship with God occurs on the human, not the divine level."[1] According to Luther, the incarnation—God descending to humans in creation for their justification—was not only the historical locus of God's saving act in Christ but the para-digm of all theology. God encounters, calls, blesses, judges, and saves humans in creation, not apart from or beyond it on some spiritual or divine plane.

Luther's view of the incarnation determined his mature teachings on the means of grace (i.e., the ways God shows favor). God was in all things, said Luther, but what differentiated the means of grace was God's promise attached to a particular thing; in these instances, God was not just present but present *for you*. Thus Luther confessed in the *Large Catechism*, the sacrament "is the true body and blood of the Lord Christ, in and under the bread and wine."[2] But "how Christ is brought into the bread," Luther was not ashamed to admit, "I do not know."[3]

Because God meets humans in creation for their salvation, the bur-den of proof, said Luther, was on those who rejected the plain meaning of Christ's words: "This is my body . . . this is my blood . . . for the forgiveness of sins" (Matt 26:26, 28). According to Luther, one only looked for a way around Christ's clear teaching, and thus "tortured" the Scriptures, if one took offense at the thought of God being in cre-ation.[4] Such attempts were motivated by a belief that "flesh" and "spirit" were distinct essences, with "spirit" being the higher or more divine, while for Luther, "'spiritual' must mean what the Spirit does and what comes from the Spirit."[5] The devaluation of material things had dire consequences, said Luther. Those who saw the Supper as a symbol for stirring pious memory turned the sacrament into a human work rather than a divine gift. And those who affirmed Christ's spiritual presence while denying his bodily presence were guilty of separating the divine and human natures of Christ—a position that rendered the incarnation meaningless. In fact, those who desired to have God in "nothing but spirit" were left only "with the devil, who has neither flesh nor bone."[6] Instead, said Luther, "where you place God for me, you must also place the humanity for me."[7]

God's presence through Christ in creation established, for Luther, the principle that "the Spirit cannot be with us except in material and physical things."[8] This included the proclamation of God's word. The creatureliness of the word of God led Luther to speak of preaching itself as a type of incarnation. "Yes, I hear the sermon," said Luther, "but who is speaking? The minister? No, indeed! You do not hear the minister. True the voice is his; but my God is speaking the word which he preaches or speaks."[9] Luther had no problem putting Christ himself in the mouth of the preacher.

This insistence that God encountered humans on the human level also guided Luther's theology of the call to ministry. For Luther, the external call through appropriate human channels constituted a call to ministry in its entirety. "When you are called to the ministry," advised Luther, "you should consider the voice of the community as the voice of God, and obey."[10] As Luther's ordination service (1539) exhorted the ordinand,

> You must believe for certain that you were called by God, because the church sent you here and secular authority has called and desired you. For what the church and secular authorities do in these matters, God does through them, so that you may not be considered intruders.[11]

Since God spread the gospel through these human means, "if we emphasize the matter of call," claimed Luther, "we can worry the devil."[12] Conversely, "He who preaches without [the call] 'beats the air' and glories in fruit existing only in his own foolish imagination."[13] Although the ceremony of ordination was beneficial for good order, the external call *was* the authority to preach. This was especially true when the call came from a congregation, although as Wilhelm Maurer put it, "The legal form of a call makes little difference to Luther."[14] Even without ordination by a bishop (the Catholic standard of the day), a minister "is confirmed anyway by virtue of the congregation's call."[15]

The authority of the call rested in God's word. Given equally to all, the word of God established the Christian community, whose members all received the priesthood, the functions of which consist of teaching, preaching, baptizing, administering the Eucharist, binding and loosing sins, praying for others, sacrificing, and judging doctrine.[16] However, a congregation of public ministers would result in chaos, and "no one individual can arise by his own authority and arrogate to himself alone what belongs to all."[17] Thus for the sake of order, this community must designate one or more of its members to the office of public ministry on its behalf. In this way, Luther maintained the distinction not between "lay" and "clergy," as is often assumed, but between being Christian in general and the ministerial office.[18] For Luther, a call was particular to a setting. He believed those called as "teachers" (i.e., with a teaching post) were called to proclaim truth and refute error everywhere.[19] But a regular minister with a valid call in one locale had no absolute right to minister somewhere else, even if false teachings were being promulgated there.[20] For this reason, Luther warned against wandering preachers who were "unable to produce their authorization."[21]

According to Luther, an inner call could be valid in two circumstances. First, an inner call ought to "be proved with miraculous signs." God may indeed directly call preachers, but without signs attesting to the call, "one can believe no one who relies on his own spirit and inner feelings for authority and who outwardly storms against God's accustomed order."[22] Luther considered such miraculous verification to be a fulfillment of the biblical mandate for two or more witnesses:

> As you boast of the Spirit, give me proof. You bear witness of yourself, and the Scriptures have forbidden me to believe you on your own testimony alone, for even Christ, the living Son of God would not bear witness of himself, as we read in the Gospel of John 5:31f. But when he did so he also did miracles besides, so that men might know that his Word and doctrine were true. And inasmuch as you say you have the Holy Spirit, give me a proof of your Spirit; prove it by real signs that a man may believe you, for here a divine witness is necessary to prove the Spirit of God, so that there may be two of you, yourself and God. This is a divine call, and unless it is forthcoming, cast the other away and let it go to pieces.[23]

So crucial was this divine witness that Luther advised believers even to reject the ministry of any self-proclaimed inwardly (or immediately) called preacher who had a right spirit and doctrine but lacked miracles as proof of God's call. After all, "the devil can preach too." In judging such "self-called" preachers, the question is not "what you preach, but whether you are sent."[24] God, who may test the faithful by sending preachers with a "true spirit" without a true call, would be pleased that his children obeyed his command to insist on two witnesses.[25] In the spirit of 1 Corinthians 14, Luther felt that good order may restrain the proclamation of God's true word—although it may never silence it.

Second, a kind of inner call may operate when one finds oneself in a region lacking any other Christians or capable preachers. In this circumstance, one may be certain "he needs no other call than to be a Christian, called and anointed by God from within." This call, Luther explained, was simply the realization that "the duty of brotherly love" compelled a Christian to share the gospel where no others could.[26] One may logically conclude that this was a circumstance (although

for Luther, the *only* circumstance) in which an inner call was necessary, but such a distinction is functionally irrelevant given that it was a
call that only became effective in obvious outward circumstances and
equally applied to all Christians. "Any Christian should feel obligated
to act," said Luther, "if he saw the need and was competent to fill it, even
without a call from the community."[27] But even in the case of a lack of
preachers (but not Christians), it was better for the faithful to designate
a minister, "to commit by common vote such an office to one or more, to
be exercised in its stead."[28]

Not surprisingly, Luther did not think those in his own day who
claimed or based their authority to minister on an internal call met the
above conditions. Luther regarded them all as false prophets, "all too
highly spiritualized for me." The refuge of Satan's emissaries was the
endless unverified appeal to the Holy Spirit, while Luther quipped, "I
myself cannot boast very much of the Spirit." Such wolves bragged of
a Spirit that supposedly offered clandestine authorization to preachers, but Luther countered, "I boast of a Spirit of love."[29] Eminently
dependent on God's external means, Luther was proud to "hear no
heavenly voice."[30]

Luther especially reprimanded his former Wittenberg colleague
Andreas Karlstadt. Luther believed Karlstadt both ran from his legitimate call at Wittenberg and illegitimately placed himself in the pulpit
at Orlamünde, all in deference to what Karlstadt claimed was his "inner
call." Luther's understanding and representation of Karlstadt's actions
were not always fair or reliable, yet Luther's impressions of Karlstadt's
behavior revealed and refined important elements of Luther's doctrine of ministerial call.[31] For Luther, the appeal to an inner call was
inherently unstable, as revealed by Karlstadt's later acquiescence to
return to Wittenberg.[32] Karlstadt was probably in a no-win situation,
for Luther likely would have castigated Karlstadt for stubbornness had
he not agreed to return. Yet Luther's point was clear: ministry was service performed at the request of the proper authorities, and the inner
call was not a sufficiently stable rubric for the minister or God's flock.

Karlstadt's stress on the inner call, said Luther, led him to "preach and write when no one has commanded or requested him to do so, and when he is requested to do so, he does not do it."[33] In Karlstadt, Luther saw all his concerns about the inner call confirmed.

According to Luther, the glory of the gospel is that God comes to humans in creation. Driven by this incarnation principle, Luther believed that present-day ministers receive a "mediated call," externally, through the church—either a congregation or a representative of the church. Luther believed an "immediate call" (including an inner call) was possible but valid only when accompanied by signs. He railed against those who claimed an inner or immediate call, not only because they failed to produce the necessary signs but because they used their understanding of the call to act as unaccountable free agents.

ANDREAS KARLSTADT

Andreas Karlstadt was an ardent early supporter of Luther. But Karlstadt was also his own theologian, as became clear with his handling of reform while Luther was in exile at the Wartburg Castle in 1521–22. Sensing their agendas were at odds, Karlstadt left Wittenberg, landing at Orlamünde in 1523 in hopes of implementing his own plan for reformation.

Karlstadt's understanding of ministerial call must be understood in the context of his dismay at Catholic leaders' greed for church positions as avenues for wealth and power rather than expressions of spiritual concern. Karlstadt's highly spiritualized (i.e., interiorized) doctrine of the call was his antidote for such worldly motives and outcomes. Theologically speaking, however, Karlstadt's theory of call aligns with his rejection of externals as channels for God's grace. Karlstadt rejected the notion of Christ's bodily presence in the sacrament, believing that it distracted worshippers from the centrality of the historic cross. And because he believed spiritual realities could only be mediated by spirit, Karlstadt refused to acknowledge grace given in the elements of bread and wine. "The sacrament," said Karlstadt, "is much too coarse to touch the ground of the soul. . . . The sacrament cannot assure our spirit and help the weakness of our spirit. . . . The assurance belongs to God's Spirit, not to any creature."[34] Instead, the elements were signifiers of spiritual realities aiding in "remembrance."[35] Karlstadt argued that the internal experience of remembrance was the only proper means of encountering grace. To be sure, this was not simple mental recollection but "a fresh, ardent, and powerful remembrance" that brought joy and conformed the partaker to Christ.[36] The benefit of the Supper, according to Karlstadt, even occurred for communicants who would "go into [their] inwardness" and "feel an experience" *before* partaking.[37] Likewise, hearing God's external word was incidental to inner revelation and the experience of grace, as Karlstadt believed such awakening could happen apart from physical hearing.[38]

While at Orlamünde and after nearly a year of silence in the face of Luther's attacks, Karlstadt wrote a personal defense. He chastised his flock, claiming they had approached him "unwisely" in asking him to speak before the Spirit moved him.[39] The fact that they had called him to serve as a minister was irrelevant, since such "a human and external sending . . . may well be worthless in God's sight; indeed, it may even be opposed to God." Unmoved by the explicit concerns of his followers and their request for instruction, Karlstadt saw the human request as potentially harmful. "In truth," wrote Karlstadt, "such a human call is a dangerous and deceptive pledge[,] and to depend on human calling is presumptuous and wanton if God's inner call is not added to assure inwardly the one who is called with this imprinted seal and sure pledge."[40] For Karlstadt, the external call was unstable and unreliable, vulnerable to the whims of the masses.

Conversely, Karlstad described the "precious, sure, and essential" inner calling as that which "gives truthful testimony that the one who is called is a servant of the Lord God whose little sheep they are." Luther used passages in John 10 to argue that ministers were subject to the community, but for Karlstadt, these same passages showed that an internal call was necessary. "Whoever has found this [inner calling] to be true and rightly understands it enters by the door," argued Karlstadt. "But the one who cannot discern the calling enters by climbing the wall." The best course for a would-be preacher, claimed Karlstadt, was "to be silent and wait until God—whom no power can resist—prods."[41]

The congregation bore responsibility in discerning the inner call in a potential minister. Rather than "trust in its own will and intention," advised Karlstadt, the congregation "should first know the persons and discern and understand God's inner call." Therefore, said Karlstadt, the congregation "must rigorously and seriously enquire about the divine secret calling with great diligence and serious prayer and sincere sighs." Furthermore, the congregation needed its own inner call—that is, an internal testimony of the rightness of a person for the work of ministry.[42]

Karlstadt did not think that "discerning" the inner call in another person was difficult unless one "does not know God's Spirit or scripture." Nor was he interested in laying out a method or test for the minister's inner call—other than to say it was not conveyed in visions or dreams. Quite simply, for Karlstadt, the one with a true inner call has "learned to know God's will and mind and that God has chosen him." This minister "discerns such power of the word of God within himself."[43]

Karlstadt assumed the superiority of the internal and spiritual over the external and material. According to Karlstadt, an inner call was necessary and validated an external call, while an external call lacking internal confirmation was worthless and dangerous.

PHILIP MELANCHTHON: THE LUTHERAN CONFESSIONS

Due to the circumstances that led to their creation, the works included in the *Book of Concord* (1580) as standards of Lutheran theology do not directly address the inner call. Still, these documents—especially those written by Luther's Wittenberg colleague Philip Melanchthon—fill out the Lutheran understanding of ministerial call. For instance, Melanchthon's *Treatise on the Power and Primacy of the Pope* (1537) identified the arena of discussion in ministerial call as the proper external authority.

While bishops had the power of ordination, this was "by human right," subject to the bishops' faithfulness to God's word. But

> when the regular bishops become enemies of the gospel or are unwilling to ordain, the churches retain the right to do so. For wherever the church exists, there also is the right to administer the gospel. Therefore it is necessary for the church to retain the right to call, choose, and ordain ministers.[44]

Melanchthon reasoned from the gospel rather than the church hierarchy. The gospel creates the church, and "where the true church is, there must also be the right of ordaining ministers, just as in an emergency even a layperson grants absolution and becomes the minister or pastor of another."[45] Human traditions of choosing, calling, and ordaining ministers (i.e., various mechanisms of external calling) may stand so long as they serve the proclamation of God's free grace. But the right fundamentally lies with the church and reverts in practice to the true church when human traditions fail to provide faithful ministers.

Melanchthon's assumptions were as much at odds with those who championed the inner call as with those who insisted on ordination by bishops. When threatened with the unfaithfulness of the Catholic clergy, Melanchthon did not, like Karlstadt, interiorize the call to protect the ministry from worldly abuse. The church, which is the "assembly of believers" (article 7 of the Augsburg Confession), is a community; it holds the right of call always in service to the gospel but also as a *communal gift*. For this reason, the confessions recognized no call to ministry that is individualized, interior, or secret.

A related line of thought in the confessions also implied a critique of the inner call theory. So completely characterized by its service in the external means of God's grace, the ministry itself might be seen as a means of grace. In this light, Melanchthon had "no objection to calling ordination a sacrament." He went on in article 13 of the *Apology of the Augsburg Confession* to connect calling, ministry, and the giving of the Holy Spirit:

For the church has the mandate to appoint ministers, which ought to please us greatly because we know that God approves this ministry and is present in it. Indeed, it is worthwhile to extol the ministry of the Word with every possible kind of praise against fanatics who imagine that the Holy Spirit is not given through the Word but is given on account of certain preparations of their own, for example, if they sit idle and silent in dark places while waiting for illumination.[46]

That Melanchthon would "extol the ministry . . . with . . . praise," even to the point of calling ordination a sacrament, sheds crucial light on the early Lutheran doctrine of the ministry. For all parties involved, the understanding of the means of grace signaled the doctrine of call and ordination. In the Lutheran confessions, the means of grace (the sacraments) were external, and call/ordination was a means of grace; therefore, call/ordination was external. For the "fanatics" (including Karlstadt), however, means of grace were internal (since they believed the Holy Spirit comes to people apart from external channels), and call/ordination—as a fundamental aspect of ministry—in some way mediated grace (Karlstadt did not follow his logic to the conclusion of eliminating the external office of ministry altogether); therefore, call/ordination was internal.

In the Lutheran confessions, the ministry is shaped by its tools, means, and context. Just as the work of ministry centers on external word and sacrament publicly proclaimed amid a visible gathering of believers, the mechanisms that bring ministers into office are also external, public, and visible.

John Calvin

At the Marburg Colloquy of 1529, Luther could not find agreement on the nature of Christ's presence in the Lord's Supper with another branch of reformers, setting the trajectories of what would become the Lutheran and Reformed churches. Nevertheless, the Reformed theology of the Geneva reformer John Calvin was influential on Protestant theologians of many stripes, making his views on ministerial call crucial for understanding later Lutheran developments.

As with other reformers, Calvin's presuppositions about material and spiritual realms colored his whole theology. Calvin believed material means could facilitate an encounter with God, but he placed the encounter itself in the inner, spiritual, nonmaterial realm. Regarding Christ's presence in the Lord's Supper, Calvin argued that something would be "withdrawn from Christ's heavenly glory" if Christ were to be "brought under the corruptible elements of this world, or bound to any earthly creatures."[47] He, therefore, rejected the Lutheran doctrine of Christ's bodily presence in the Supper and its corollary of ubiquity (Christ's body is present everywhere). According to Calvin, Christ's body was in heaven, eternally restricted by space.[48] Calvin thought he was close to Luther on the Supper, but Calvin's friends were convinced he didn't perceive the crassness and barbarity of Luther's view.[49] Calvin did not go as far as Karlstadt's view of remembrance; instead, he said, "In the mystery of the Supper, Christ is truly shown to us through the symbols of bread and wine." However, the actual meeting place of Christ and believers was not on earth *in* the Supper but in heaven *by means* of the Supper through the work of the Holy Spirit.[50]

Calvin's reluctance to locate God's presence in material things extended also to his view of preaching. Although Calvin in several places nearly identified God's speech and human preaching, he was inclined to use qualifying phrases, like "as if" and "as though" (e.g., "proclaiming the word of God . . . as if he were speaking in us"), which had the effect of distinguishing the preached word from the presence of Christ.[51] For Calvin, the human and external element in preaching functioned chiefly as an "exercise in humility," for when hearers submit to a "puny man" as God's minister, they show "evidence of piety."[52]

Calvin's views on ministerial call aligned with his theology of the sacraments and preaching. A minister must be "duly called," said Calvin, by which he meant "the outward and solemn call which has to do with the public order of the church."[53] For Calvin, the external call "belongs to order; for God will have all things carried on by us orderly and without confusion."[54] But Calvin also explained that the calling to ministry was "twofold," with "an outer and inner call."[55] While he intended to pass over what he called the "secret call" without much comment, Calvin made a crucial move by introducing the inner call to ministry into "magisterial" Protestantism—that is, Protestantism with the backing of secular authorities. Calvin was, in fact, introducing an idea that was foreign to historic Christianity. Although monastics spoke of an internal call (see chapter 4), the phenomenon had not applied to the ministry. As Catholic scholar James Puglisi writes, "Only three realities counted in the early Church: the task to fulfill, the faith and aptitudes of the elect [the would-be minister], and the call of the Church."[56] Inner call to ministry was a sixteenth-century Protestant invention of Karlstadt and Calvin.

Calvin believed that the inner call guaranteed pure motives, "that we undertake the offered office neither from ambition nor avarice, nor any other selfish feeling, but a sincere fear of God and desire to edify the Church." Defined as "the good testimony of our heart," Calvin did not provide much direction for those coming after him who sought precision in the inner call. This call was hidden and private; it "does not have the church as witness." But neither could Calvin's heirs dismiss it, since he took for granted that "every minister is conscious [of the secret call] before God," and he argued that it was "necessary for every one of us, if we would have our ministry approved by God."[57]

Calvin discerned a dichotomy between human and divine activity: humans act in the material realm, while God acts in an unseen spiritual sphere. Therefore, "the external call," which Calvin relegated to the realm of human activity,

> is never legitimate, except it be preceded by the internal, for it
> does not belong to us to create prophets, or apostles, or pastors,
> as this is the special work of the Holy Spirit. Though then one
> be called and chosen by men a hundred times, he cannot yet

be deemed a legitimate minister, except he has been called by God. . . . We hence see that the hidden call of God is ever necessary, in order that one may become a prophet, or an apostle, or a pastor.[58]

According to Calvin, the Holy Spirit was responsible for the inner call but not the external call. Calvin thus made the external call dependent on a hidden internal "testimony."

For Calvin, God's saving activity involved created elements, but its true locus was inward, unseen, operating in the realm of the Spirit (or heaven). This was true of Christ in the Supper and Christ's activity in preaching. Calvin consistently applied this presupposition by teaching that the ministry, too, rested on a secret inner call.

LUTHERAN ORTHODOXY

As the impulses of Lutheranism became institutionalized, theologians in the generations after Luther worked to preserve its teachings, answer criticism, and explain points of difference from other traditions. From the late 1500s through the early 1700s, these mostly German theologians created what scholars call Lutheran "orthodoxy." In their efforts to provide clarity, precision, and organization to their writings, orthodox theologians increasingly relied on philosophical categories and language, in general bearing the stamp of Melanchthon's fastidiousness rather than Luther's dynamism. They treated the ministerial call with the meticulousness they applied to every other theological topic. Less customarily, one in their ranks opened the door for an understanding of the inner call that had no support in Luther or the Lutheran confessions.

The Nature and Purpose of the Call

Grounded in article 14 of the Augsburg Confession, the orthodox writers insisted on the necessity of a regular call for ministry. God calls ministers to proclaim the gospel so that sinners might be justified on account of Christ. A call was "regular" or "legitimate" in the sense that it was public and conformed to Scripture. For Johann Gerhard, a legitimate call was necessary because (1) God ordained and willed it, (2) hearers could thereby be certain about their ministers and God's presence in their ministries, and (3) ministers derived confidence and comfort from it.[59] As Johann Andreas Quenstedt said, "The call of God makes the work legitimate, and one who has not been called by God cannot rightly and properly perform the office." Legitimacy of office was not to be confused with correctness of teaching, however. Errors or false teaching did not mean an illegitimate call, and neither did a legitimate call ensure pure teaching.[60]

Like Luther, orthodox writers insisted that ministry should not cease in circumstances that might not allow for a traditional call, such as being the only Christian in a region. But the orthodox understood this somewhat differently than Luther, who argued that the common baptismal call authorized ministry in such circumstances. Quenstedt, however, refused to regard the Christian who ministers "where the church is still to be gathered" as having a call at all.[61]

Types of Call: Immediate and Mediate

The chief distinction for Lutheran orthodox writers on ministerial call was God's *method* of calling. God called in two ways, which the orthodox treated as mutually exclusive: "immediately" (i.e., speaking directly to a person) and "mediately" (i.e., speaking through other creatures).[62] Quenstedt contrasted the Lutheran position to the Calvinist doctrine of call, which he believed to be a "third kind" that combined elements of both.[63] The immediate-mediate distinction had spatial implications: the "hearing" of an immediate call may occur internally (or be accompanied by "inner impulses"), while a mediate call was always external.[64] As such, the notion of an inner call was often in the background when the orthodox discussed the immediate call. Leonhard Hutter summarized the distinction:

One [call is the] immediate or direct call, as was the call of the prophets and apostles, which was given by God himself without employment of any means, and which ceased with the prophets and apostles; the other [is] a mediate call, such as is now given by the church, which consists of the higher powers or government, the ministers of the church, and the remaining hearers, commonly called the people or laity.[65]

As Hutter suggested, the immediate call was not typical of the post-biblical age, although some orthodox followed Luther in allowing the possibility of present-day immediate calls so long as they were accompanied by miraculous signs.[66] Hutter's summary also indicated the orthodox teachers' specific conception of the "church," through which a mediate call came. Secular rulers, ministers, and the laity all had roles in the process. The orthodox strove for balance in maintaining the voice of the whole church in ministerial call.[67]

Although the potential minister heard the mediate call delivered *through* other people, he was to regard it as being *from* God. The mediate call, according to Martin Chemnitz, enjoyed "the same promises of divine grace and efficacy" as the immediate call.[68] In asserting the divine origin of the mediate call, Chemnitz felt compelled to insist that it was not necessary "only for the sake of order," suggesting an uneasiness with associating human mechanisms too closely with God's activity.[69] This was a subtle but important departure from Luther. Chemnitz and Quenstedt further argued that the immediate call was superior to the mediate call in dignity and divine gifts.[70]

Despite the glory of the immediate call, orthodox teachers echoed Luther's hostility toward present-day claims to the experience. They argued that God had not commanded postbiblical-era believers to look for or promised to supply ministers through an immediate call.[71] Furthermore, said Gerhard, there was no longer a need for the immediate call, since God had prescribed a clear method for establishing ministry by the mediate call and promised to sustain ministry to the end of the age.[72] By contrast, orthodox thinkers continued to associate contemporary claims of an immediate call with Anabaptists. It was not a favorable association:

> By the revelation of the Enthusiasts (1) the order of the ministry, or the order among teachers and learners divinely established in the church, is overturned; (2) the ranks set up in the Christian church are mixed up; (3) the certainty of faith is destroyed; (4) the door is opened to some impersonators [and] imposters and their heresies and errors.[73]

According to the orthodox, claims of an immediate call tended to lack accountability, eroding order and the reliability of ministry. Given these dangers—and the fact that the mediate call was equally effective, had the benefit of being surer, and had the distinction of being divinely promised—they believed the immediate call to be extremely rare (if not extinct) and valid only when accompanied by publicly verifiable testimony from God.

Opening the Door to Inner Call

The general attitude of the orthodox in dismissing the immediate call did not mean that a person's experience leading to ministry lacked an internal dimension. Chemnitz, for instance, granted that a person may desire to serve as a minister and that God may move upon a person in any decision-making process. But this, he maintained, is not the same as having a call.[74] Gerhard was willing to attribute more but still greatly qualified value to the internal aspects of ministry. When rejecting the Catholic claim that the early church's language of "divine chrism" referred to outward anointing in ordination, Gerhard insisted the phrase rather referred to the minister's "inner anointing of the Holy Spirit."[75] Responding to the Calvinist Gulielmus Bucanus's claim that all true ministers have a "hidden" call through the Holy Spirit, Gerhard conceded "that by internal impulse and inspiration God does inspire in some people this intent to undertake the ecclesiastical ministry." He further noted that ministers are required to be "led by sincere love for God and concern for building the church." If people wanted to refer to a God-placed desire for ministry and the requirement for godly motivations as a "hidden call," said Gerhard, "we will not resist it too much."[76]

This was not a full-throated endorsement of Calvinist terminology. In fact, Gerhard objected to Calvinist claims that corrupt motives invalidated an otherwise legitimate call and that the inner dispositions of the minister somehow constituted part of the call. But he was not direct about this. Gerhard's relative comfort with the language of "inner confirmation," "inner anointing," and "hidden call" suggests that Calvinist approaches to ministerial call were making inroads into Lutheran thinking.

RELATION TO SACRAMENTAL THEOLOGY

In broad strokes, the orthodox were faithful followers of Luther's view of God's relation to creation. They recognized God's voice in preaching and absolution and insisted on the bodily presence of Christ in the Lord's Supper.[77] Chemnitz, however, was uncomfortable with Luther's extreme form of ubiquity, preferring the notion that Christ is present everywhere *as he wills* rather than by sheer consequence of the union of divine and human natures, leading to what one scholar calls "an uncertainty of whether Christ was *really* present everywhere, according to his human nature, or if he was merely *potentially* omnipresent." Through the *Formula of Concord* (1577), Chemnitz bequeathed this uncertainty to later orthodox theologians.[78]

While these distinctions may seem to deal with arcane debates about Christology, Chemnitz's doctrine revealed a subtle yet telling uneasiness with the notion of material things bearing divinity. In other theologians, this uneasiness, as we have seen, correlated to a doctrine of the inner call to ministry. Although Chemnitz may not have had much room for the notion of the inner call, Gerhard, who was influenced by Chemnitz's qualified doctrine of Christ's omnipresence, did.

LUTHERANISM OF THE HEART

An "eclectic Lutheran spirituality" developed alongside orthodoxy, showing less strict adherence to the *Book of Concord* and incorporating a range of ideas from beyond the boundaries of Lutheranism.[79] These writers emphasized Christian practice and the psychological experience of relationship with God—what they often called "the inner life." Many had a mystical streak and bemoaned the viciousness of theological dispute among Lutherans. Some took a prophetic role, decrying what they viewed as an overreliance on correct doctrine and participation in the sacraments. Others—whom historians have mostly ignored—were systematic academic theologians who examined correct doctrine and the inner life with equal zeal. Because of their idiosyncrasies, we will explore some key thinkers in turn.

FOUNDATIONS: JOHANN ARNDT

Johann Arndt, a pastor in Quedlinburg, was fascinated with the interior life:

> Faith is the means of attaining our inward treasure, when God holds a still Sabbath and a man turns within himself. For just as the motion of the heavenly bodies is, there, the most noble and perfect, because it returns to the origin from which it began its course: so also the life journey of man may be accounted most noble and perfect, when it returns to its origin, which is God. But this cannot happen unless a man goes within himself with all his powers, withdraws his understanding, will, and memory from the world and all fleshly things, turns his soul with all its desires to God through the Holy Spirit, flees from the world and rests in the still Sabbath, which God can cause to take place within him.[80]

For Arndt, the deepest and most certain religious experience was located "within" the believer. Although he held explicitly orthodox views on Christ's presence in the Lord's Supper and respected the external means of grace, these positions were disconnected from his task of bringing sinners to an inner experience of grace:[81] "Even if you heard ten sermons every day, went to confession every month, went to receive the Lord's supper, none of this would help you unless you had the forgiveness of sins."[82] Further, for Arndt, vocations were not vehicles of devotion and obedience, as Luther saw them, but potential obstacles to spiritual progress.[83]

Arndt had great esteem for the external call to ministry, which sustained him amid ministerial hardships and transitions.[84] But under Arndt's influence, the ordination of ministers began to emphasize the importance of the candidate's *intention*. This can be seen in the words of the 1657 ordination liturgy of Braunschweig-Wolfenbüttel:

> In so far as you are resolved from your heart and with conviction
> to carry out this office, bear witness to it with your affirmative
> response, given you by God, in the presence of the omniscient
> God and his church: After that the ordinand responds yes and
> means it with his whole heart.[85]

The interiorized spirituality of Arndt led to the growing acceptance of the notion that ministerial call substantially involved inner experience. Up to this point, Lutheran liturgies stressed that Christ called ministers "through members of the church."[86] Flowing with the currents of Arndtian piety, some Lutherans edged closer to the Reformed, who emphasized the mind, will, feeling, and inward inspiration of the potential minister.[87]

SYSTEMATIC THEOLOGIANS

Movement in the Reformed direction was overt in Paul Tarnow, who was part of a transitional movement, especially in Rostock, Germany, that "combined Arndtian piety, strict orthodoxy, and a deep concern for immorality and the failings of the church."[88] In his 1624 book on ministry, Tarnow argued that "the interior call [to ministry] is the divine drawing out, of which each minister is conscious before God." Equating this call with "the testimony of a good heart" and the absence of selfish motives, Tarnow approvingly cited the "secret call" in Calvin's *Institutes* along with the Italian Reformed theologian Girolamo Zanchi, who claimed that one who lacks this testimony should not be considered called by God. This "good conscience," said Tarnow, is necessary for one to be "truly conscious, if the call be from God." Although people often say men with aptitude, learning, and piety are "called," Tarnow argued that this was not the same as an internal call, and if one who were lacking in the true internal call be called by the church, these attributes are "not enough to free his conscience."[89] Tarnow was exceptional among Lutherans for his willingness to consider Calvin and other Reformed thinkers authorities, his insistence that the inner call was necessary, and his willingness to bind the potential minister's conscience to an inner call.

Despite his reputation as a champion of orthodoxy, Johann Friedrich Mayer went further than any Lutheran theologian before him in endorsing the inner call. According to his lengthy treatment in *Study of the Ministry of the Church* (1690), "If one wishes to enjoy the solace and glory of a legitimate call, it is necessary that . . . he first be certain of the internal call." Mayer identified two characteristics of the internal call: inclination and anointing. Leaning on Bernard of Clairvaux's description of the "inward impulse of charity" that spurs ministerial work, Mayer wrote that inclination is "the intimate and burning affection . . . the movement of the secret heart and joy of Spirit for the ministerial work." Such love for the work, according to Mayer, means disregarding one's own well-being for a singular focus on service and "flows from pursuit of divine glory only and the promotion of the neighbor's salvation" rather than "ambition, wealth, selfishness, and other worldly causes." Furthermore, this inclination must be a "constant impetus, impulse, and desire, not momentary, flighty, lukewarm [or] fading." On the other hand, the internal anointing of the Spirit is the combination

of "sufficient learning and necessary gifts for the ministry of the word."
Such gifts are apparent especially in the ability to teach God's word.
When the inclination and anointing are present—and Mayer said
God's will is not obscure—one cannot resist the inner call without
damaging the conscience.[90]

Rostock theologian Johann Fecht built on the work of Tarnow but
with much less detail and insistence than Mayer. For Fecht, the "natural impulse is the internal call of God," but the inclination must be
"ordered" rather than a blind zeal and consist chiefly of desire to serve
God and win souls. Nor was inclination sufficient but must be accompanied by aptitude before one considers devoting himself to theological
study. Furthermore, the desire for ministry must also include consideration of the trials and even the threat of martyrdom that accompany
the office.[91]

Pietist Reformers

In 1675, Philipp Jakob Spener wrote an introduction to a new edition of
Arndt's *True Christianity* that laid out a systematic plan for bettering the
church. Despite its measured tone, this work birthed an unprecedented
movement of spiritual zeal and earned Spener the scorn of many. From
the title of the work, *Pia Desideria* (*Pious Desires*), and Spener's proposed
mechanism for reform, the *collegia pietatis* (schools of piety), the movement took the name Pietism.

The Pietist program had implications for the view of the ministry.
One of Spener's pillars was what he called the "spiritual priesthood"—
the recognition that the laity should take an active role in spiritual
functions. Spener recognized that this emphasis was liable to misunderstanding as a license to preach and administer the sacraments
publicly without a regular call. He explained that not all Christians
are to exercise the preaching office, which "requires a *special call*."[92] In
Pia Desideria, Spener referred to Luther, who, according to Spener,
explained "that all spiritual functions are open to all Christians without exception," although "the regular and public performance of them

is entrusted to ministers appointed for this purpose."[93] Spener echoed Luther by saying, "No one is to arrogate to themselves what the entire congregation has without having a call from the congregation." However, for nonordained Christians in emergency situations, this call takes the form of a "call of love" rooted in the universal priesthood.[94]

Despite his respect for the regular external call, Spener contended that the ministry is built on more. Although the person, conduct, or character of the minister does not determine the power of God's word or validate the ministerial office, Spener insisted on the godliness and good intent of ministerial candidates, "that only such persons be called who may be suited." Anyone who fulfilled a call out of annoyance, out of pure obligation, or for any "fleshly reason" was sinning.[95] This devaluation of obligation was foreign to Luther.

Spener also argued that any particular external call was a serious matter that required diligent searching into God's will. Perhaps related to his own anxiety and indecision about his initial call to parish ministry and later invitations, Spener was concerned that ministers have an *assurance* of their divine call. Such certainty led to joy and consolation in the office. One could arrive at this certainty in many ways, but his general advice was to carefully assess one's abilities and "the inclination of the heart" and call upon God's will in submission. In this process, one "looks into the heart with God's eyes."[96] In his own experience, assurance also entailed supernatural confirmation. When he was weighing the call to Dresden, his daughter randomly opened the Scriptures, laying her thumb on Stephen's recounting in Acts 7 of the command to Abraham to "leave your country . . . and go to the land that I will show you" (Acts 7:3). Spener took this as an affirmation of God's will to accept the call.[97]

For some, said Spener, this certainty also involves an inner call. Although not experiencing it himself, he advocated for the concept, saying that "many have a strong feeling of the heart and recognize the inner call within." According to Spener, God gave this experience to some who with "pious deliberation of the matter can come to a certainty in the heart and likewise feel the inner call within themselves." Even if it did not involve an inner call per se, for Spener, the assurance of one's call was a dynamic internal process. As Spener put it, "Assurance of divine call always fixes more and more in my soul." But he also recognized the potential for self-delusion in any inner experience. The "heartfelt intention" he had experienced regarding his call to Strasbourg, for instance, made it difficult to distinguish a divine call from a temptation. The possibility of error in the inner call was matched by the potential for wielding the concept to deceive others. Because of the cunning of those who have entered ministry contrary to the intent of the office, Spener advised caution when discussing the inner call.[98] In sum, Spener viewed the assurance of call as an interior experience and endorsed the inner call as one possible aspect of this assurance, but he suggested that this experience was not wholly reliable.

Many of Spener's heirs were not as practical or restrained as he was. Some radical Pietists used the stress on inner life to justify unusual messages or methods, claiming the right to prophesy or preach solely on the basis of mystical experiences. The work of these "uncalled street-corner preachers" (as their opponents called them) directly challenged the necessity or even the legitimacy of the external call.[99] But they mostly remained on the fringes. The Spener disciple who was far more influential on later views of ministerial call was August Hermann Francke.

Well known for building the institutions of social welfare and church renewal in the German city of Halle (including its new university), Francke also stressed the interior life. His account of spiritual struggle culminating in a conversion experience in 1688 in which he was "overwhelmed by a flood of joy" that dispelled all doubts and instilled "a true living faith" became a model for Pietist spirituality.[100] Francke urged believers to harmonize themselves with "the ways by which God goes inwardly and outwardly." The one who accomplishes this, said Francke, will "quiet his heart even in the midst of suffering and yield to all peace."[101]

This vision of interior experience appeared also in Francke's view of ministry. Francke drew a straight line between orthodox preachers' moral permissiveness and their lack of the experience of grace. In his controversial 1698 sermon "On False Prophets," Francke sharpened the claim that "unconverted" ministers could not be effective. This had implications for the call to ministry. From 1729, Prussia required each ministerial candidate to receive from the Halle faculty a testimonial that included an endorsement of the candidate's experience of grace. The intent was to bar those seeking only personal gain.[102]

Francke further argued that one aspect of the false minister's "sheepskin," or deceptive veneer, is the "outward calling"

> to which false prophets appeal and for that reason consider themselves servants of God and Christ, for since they have been called by the territorial authorities and now have been placed in office and now have received sign and seal, they think that they have sufficient witness that they are teachers ordained by God, even though if their conscience would be examined it would be found that they have come into office via a bad way.[103]

According to Francke, not only does the regular external call *not* ensure the validity of the ministerial call, but relying on an outward call only signals a false minister:

> It is not so much if one has a letter that one can know if he is called to the office or commissioned. . . . But one should further ask: If one is also sent by God's Spirit and through the same [Spirit] made competent to lead the office of the Spirit in power and thus be truthfully called of God and have the witness thereof in your heart.[104]

Francke's invective against "false prophets" marks several turns from his teacher Spener. First, a regular external call was not enough. This was a logical foundation for the second development: not only was the inner call (here "sent by God's Spirit" with "the witness thereof in your heart") a possible element of a true call, but it was now *necessary*. What for Spener was one acceptable factor of assurance among many became for Francke a requirement. Finally, not only did Francke add a requirement to the external call, but he actively denigrated it—at least if it were used as a basis for the certainty of God's will in the call process.

Nicolas Ludwig, count von Zinzendorf, always considered himself theologically a Lutheran. Born into a family devoted to Spener's brand of spirituality and shaped by his early education at Halle, Zinzendorf was inclined, however, to the broad theology he found in Luther's *Small Catechism* and the Augsburg Confession rather than the boundary marking of the *Formula of Concord*. His opponents criticized him as a "garden without walls" for his doctrinal fluidity and easy cooperation with Reformed, Moravian, Anabaptist, and Catholic Christians. By station and education an aristocratic statesman, Zinzendorf was at heart a minister. The mixed community that took refuge on his Saxony estate and called it Herrnhut gave him the opportunity to see himself as not just a patron or benefactor but a spiritual guide.

Although two theological faculties approved him for Lutheran ministry in 1734, and despite a lifetime of spiritual leadership, Zinzendorf never received a regular call from a congregation, community, or church organization. Frankly, he regarded such externals as incidental to his ministerial call. Zinzendorf's true call, as he saw it, was inward. From childhood, Zinzendorf believed he had a "divine call" to the ministry, which he called his "drive" or "impulse." As he wrote to his grandmother, "Life-long I have felt a great calling to lead souls to Christ rather than to pursue a worldly occupation." Zinzendorf did not pit external and internal calls against each other as Francke did, nor did he deny the efficacy of ministry of "unconverted" men. But Zinzendorf did finesse a relationship between external and internal calls that was novel at the time. During the examination before the Tübingen faculty that resulted in his endorsement, Zinzendorf said that his lifelong belief in Christ's death for the life of the world "led to a feeling, this feeling has awakened love and love has kept me busy . . . acquaint[ing] souls with the Saviour."[105] He justified his need for approval for public ministry *on the basis of* his internal call.

Zinzendorf didn't formulate a general doctrine of call from his own experience. He likely felt compelled to stress his sense of internal call because members of the nobility, like himself, were expected to attend to matters of state rather than ministry. Claiming a personal divine call helped him defend a career path that bucked societal obligations. Furthermore, Zinzendorf seemed to be making exceptions for himself when he claimed authority to preach on a strained interpretation of Stephanas's household ordaining themselves (1 Cor 16:14–18).[106]

The implications of Zinzendorf's internal call, however, reached beyond his entry into ministry. In official pronouncements, Zinzendorf stated that no one should publicly preach or administer the sacraments without a regular call.[107] But in practice, he argued that his internal call granted him freedom from ecclesiastical structures. "I reserve to myself liberty of conscience," opined the count. "It agrees with my internal call to the ministry."[108] Zinzendorf's views were complicated by his idiosyncratic understanding of denominations themselves. Not only did he regard traditions beyond Lutheranism as divinely ordained "ways of discipline," but he envisioned a spiritual entity that subsumed all denominations.[109] Thus he saw no inconsistency in being ordained as a Moravian bishop, overseeing the Lutheran constituency of the Moravian Brethren. When he later divested himself of the Moravian episcopacy, Zinzendorf communicated that "my calling, which I certainly think I have received from the Lord, and not from men, extends further [than the Moravian church]."[110] He thought of himself as a minister at large who could not be confined to one denomination or office.[111] Zinzendorf's inner call determined the form and scope of his ministry and was to stir considerable confusion among Lutherans in the North American colonies.

2 AMERICAN DEVELOPMENTS

COLONIAL AMERICA

DESPITE THEIR PIETISTIC BENT toward inner spirituality, colonial Lutherans' discussions about ministerial vocation revolved largely around external issues of authority and protocol. This is understandable considering the chaotic conditions of their work. Their churches were scattered and poor; they received inconsistent (or no) support from Europe and no state support. Frequently, churches were begun before securing ministers and attracted inept, unfit, or scandal-prone ones along with con men and others without a regular call or ordination, or both. On top of these difficulties, these immigrants had no experience with the "voluntary principle"—that is, governing churches, judging candidates' qualifications, and committing to ministers' material support.

EARLY AMERICAN LUTHERANISM

An example of early American Lutheran chaos was the so-called Tulpehocken Confusion of the 1730s.[1] In this Pennsylvania settlement of Palatine Germans, two rival pastors fought for control of the church building and the hearts of parishioners. Both had suspicious circumstances surrounding their calls and ordinations that partisans seized upon. The animosity was so great that at one point, one group was locked out of the church, prompting one follower to "cut another door" with a saw.[2] On another occasion, someone threw stones through the parsonage window.

As seen at Tulpehocken, casting aspersions on another's external call or ordination was common, yet it usually settled little. In an earlier controversy, a tailor named Johann Bernhard van Dieren claimed to be sent from London to minister to several congregations that were already served by a duly ordained and called minister. In response, Andrew Hesselius, provost of the Swedish churches in Pennsylvania, maintained Luther's admonition to "await the One who calls thee," since ministers are called despite their own desires or will.[3] Such pleadings had little effect on a mission field starving for ministers and lacking clear lines of authority or means of enforcement. Until the founding of the Ministerium of Pennsylvania in 1748, the most any authority could do was plead, as Gotthilf August Francke of Halle (son of August Hermann Francke) did with the Lutherans in Pennsylvania in 1744:

> Further, I very seriously admonish you not to take up with every-
> one who comes in his own name, professing to be a teacher. You
> know from experience, how often you have been deceived by
> such persons. Nothing is more certain than this, that those per-
> sons who, without a regular call, push themselves into the office
> of teacher, are always seeking to make gain out of you, and either
> have been deposed from pastoral office in Germany . . . or they
> were not fit to be trusted with the care of anything.[4]

Leaders often appealed to an ideal of a regular call (by which they meant an external call), but there was no agreement in the colonies as to what entity had the right to issue a regular call.

Although the external call figured large in their church struggles, early Lutherans also hinted at internal experiences connected with ministerial call. While not the searching "resolved from your heart and with conviction" of the 1657 Braunschweig-Wolfenbüttel ordination liturgy, the first Lutheran ordination in America displayed a similar concern about the candidate's intentions: "Do you," the suffragan asked Justus Falckner in 1703, "declare yourself *willing* to undertake this holy ministerial office in the name of the holy Trinity?"[5] As one German candidate being considered for a call to New York wrote to the Hamburg Ministerium in 1724, "I have come to regard the many inner promptings as truly divine signs of a call."[6] Likewise, the Halle authorities told the churches in Pennsylvania in 1744 that candidate Peter Brunnholtz "recognized the will of God" in the external call to serve their congregations, claiming that "God Himself deeply convinced his heart that such [a call] was the Divine will."[7] Lutherans associated with the early colonial churches occasionally appealed to the inward dimensions of the call to ministry, even if they were not fully articulating it as an "inner call."

HENRY MELCHIOR MUHLENBERG
AND THE MINISTERIUM OF PENNSYLVANIA

The United Congregations of Pennsylvania (Philadelphia, Trappe [Providence], and New Hanover) requested a minister from Halle repeatedly beginning in 1735. However, it did not consent to Francke's conditions that the congregations accept and submit to any minister Halle sent, commit to a regular pastor's salary in cash, and allow the minister to leave for any reason (and even pay his fare back to Europe if he wished to leave!). Instead, the United Congregations began looking to the Darmstadt Consistory for a minister in 1739.[8] When the Moravian threat reached a fever pitch in 1742 with the arrival of Zinzendorf (who had fallen out of favor with Halle), Halle sent Henry Melchior Muhlenberg to the United Congregations—despite the fact that the two sides never came to an agreement on terms and the United Congregations earlier informed Halle that they would request ministers from elsewhere.[9] The tireless organizational work of this "Halle man" would earn him the title of "patriarch of American Lutheranism."

As with earlier colonial Lutheran controversies, the issue of a proper external call to ministry was forefront in the confrontation between Zinzendorf and Muhlenberg in Philadelphia on December 30, 1742. Zinzendorf—who obtained a call from the Lutheran church in Philadelphia that remained strangely unsigned—styled himself as a general apostle filling a leadership void; Halle and Muhlenberg painted him as an unorthodox, unaccountable sheep stealer. When Muhlenberg wrested control of the Lutheran congregations, the letter of call issued to him repudiated any "such a Minister which is not lawfull called, neither Sent or ordained according to the 14 Articul of the Augsbourg Confession."[10] The language was clearly aimed at Zinzendorf's ministry.

This scene might demonstrate, as some have suggested, that colonial Lutheranism consistently defended the need for a legitimate external call. But two factors complicate this. First, although Muhlenberg took the external call very seriously, he did not have a clear and consistent notion of what it entailed. In the chaotic field of the colonies, such clarity and consistency were probably impossible. To some degree, this was a matter of perceived jurisdiction. Trusting that his call was to the United Congregations of Pennsylvania, Muhlenberg demurred when the congregation at Hackensack (New Jersey) asked for his input in calling a minister.[11] Yet in Pennsylvania, Muhlenberg used the ministerium as a tool to grasp control over ministerial call and dismissal from congregations.[12] In other instances, Muhlenberg's varying approach was related to confessional boundaries and asserting the authority of Halle. As a few examples, Muhlenberg interfered with the work of Lawrence Nyberg (a Lutheran pastor with an unassailable call but Moravian leanings), strong-armed a Halle colleague into the Lancaster Lutheran pulpit over the objections of its council, and foisted a layperson as pastor on a Lutheran congregation in Tulpehocken.[13] Likewise, Muhlenberg laid great stress on his and his ministerium colleagues' regular call when refuting the accusation from Nyberg that "Hallensians are Pietists and not real Lutherans."[14]

In short, the "regular call" was, for Muhlenberg, a helpfully ill-defined tool useful in combatting rivals.

Second, for all the stress Muhlenberg placed on the external call, he did not see it as sufficient. As with most Pietists, Muhlenberg doubted the effectiveness of ministers who lacked an experience of grace. Such "unconverted teachers," said Muhlenberg, can't deal with the potential problems caused by awakenings.[15] According to Muhlenberg, "Whoever ordains or admits unconverted men to the office of minister of the word will have to answer for it when he goes to meet his God in eternity."[16]

Muhlenberg narrowly avoided the heresy of denying the validity of an impure minister's work, arguing that an unawakened minister was not thereby worthless or necessarily harmful.[17] And he also urged congregations to be forgiving and understanding of ministers' "human faults and weaknesses."[18] Yet in the process of decrying unconverted or immoral ministers, Muhlenberg articulated several necessary elements of the ministerial call:

> But how does it come to pass that such worshippers of the belly ever get into the holy office? Who has called them? God has not called them, neither has He ordained them. Jesus Christ, the faithful lover of souls, employs in such holy services only those who truly love Him, and for whom He Himself has done so much that they hold Him to be their highest good. The man whom God puts into the office of the ministry has to have a threefold call: 1. A pastor and teacher must have natural gifts, proportioned to the work in which God intends to use him; 2. He must have spiritual gifts; 3. He must be mediately called and chosen by the church.[19]

Although Muhlenberg characterized the call as "threefold"—natural gifts, spiritual gifts, and the external call—the requirement that ministers be those who "truly love" God seems to be a fourth element.

In speaking of the pioneer Lutheran ministers who came to America before him, Muhlenberg gloried, "They had the satisfaction of possessing a regular call, for . . . nothing but love for their Saviour and His wandering sheep would have moved them to accept the call to this wilderness with its sufferings and tribulations."[20] Muhlenberg suggested that their devotion was evidence of their "regular call."

As we've seen, earlier Lutherans considered personal qualifications such as gifts and devotion part of the inner call. Muhlenberg didn't make this explicit connection, but the effect of classifying personal characteristics as part of the "call" in addition to the external call of the church was the same. Regardless, he also endorsed more overt inner call language. In the first ordination performed by the Ministerium of Pennsylvania (the same year as its first meeting, 1748), Muhlenberg and his colleagues questioned the candidate, John Kurtz, about "the internal and external guidings that he has experienced," including "the reasons for his devoting himself to the office of the ministry of the Gospel."[21] Kurtz thereafter described how, around the age of twenty, "I felt an impulse urging me to be more earnest and resolute in serving the Lord."[22] At this same meeting, Muhlenberg protested that rival preachers "have neither an inner nor an external call."[23] What Muhlenberg meant by "inner call" and how he determined whether someone had it are unclear. But what is clear is that he felt it was important.

As part of a transatlantic awakening of "heart religion," colonial Lutherans' Pietism may have carried the influence of leading evangelical thinkers of the time. For instance, John Wesley, founder of the Methodists, and Isaac Backus, influential New England Baptist, both made passionate cases for the necessity of an inner call.[24] The fact that Muhlenberg and other colonial Lutherans did not feel compelled to explain or justify their appeals to "inner call," "inner promptings," or the emphasis on a candidate's willingness to undertake ministry suggests that it was an uncontroversial aspect of ministerial call perhaps rooted in the widespread concern that the churches have leaders entering ministry from pure motives. Consumed by the pressing needs of establishing churches in a new land, these leaders also lacked the time and resources to put their views down in a systematic form. This would change as American Lutheranism entered its age of definition in the nineteenth century.

AMERICANISTS AND CONFESSIONALISTS

Muhlenberg had planted churches, ordained ministers, and organized leadership structures, but he left no distinct theological stamp. The generation after his death in 1792 lacked systematic theological thought and saw a decline of commitment to the Lutheran confessions. Through the better part of the nineteenth century, however, Lutherans in America labored to define their faith with growing, although uneven, zeal for the confessions. The doctrine of the inner call to ministry corroborates these generalizations. Lutherans in the early republic considered an inner call normal but did not bother to explain it in detail. But as the nineteenth century progressed, leaders described and defined the inner call with increasing elaboration.

"AMERICAN LUTHERANISM"

Lutherans who took the lead in establishing institutions and crafting theology for the American context believed that Lutheranism was not a set of sixteenth-century doctrines but the principles of religious progress and private judgment based on individual rationality. They claimed for their project the name "American Lutheranism." Their leader was Samuel Simon Schmucker, who founded, led, and taught for four decades at Gettysburg Seminary in Pennsylvania, the first stable Lutheran theological seminary in America. Schmucker was also instrumental in the success of the General Synod, the first national Lutheran body in America. Schmucker returned the Augsburg Confession to the consciousness of Lutherans in America, but he believed it contained several "errors" and thus was a useful but not literally binding tool in the quest for greater theological clarity.

At a time when many ministers entered their work with little train-ing, education, or oversight, leaders became increasingly concerned with ministerial qualifications, often to the point of conflating qualifi-cations with ministerial call. Simeon Harkey, a student of Schmucker, argued that "a minister must be a truly converted and devotedly pious man." Harkey claimed that an unconverted man "has no business in the ministry . . . for [God] does not call unconverted men."[25] An *Evan-gelical Review* article in 1860 argued that "true tests of a call to minis-try" included piety, prayerfulness, "passion for the work" (enthusiasm, dedication, perseverance, and right motives), "a well-balanced mind," intelligence, education, and a strong character. "Are [our own powers] equal to the duties and demands of the office which we contemplate?" asked the writer. "This is to be regarded as the Scriptural call, as the Divine indication, that a man is authorized to preach the Gospel."[26] The highly personal nature of ministerial call was also evident in the explicit discussions of the inner call. Schmucker's *Elements of Popu-lar Theology* (1834) offered the first attempt in the English language to define the inner call from a Lutheran perspective. Conveying notions he had imbibed under Presbyterian theologian Samuel Miller at Prince-ton Theological Seminary, Schmucker wrote that "the regular call may be divided into internal and external. By the former is meant the con-viction of the individual that God has designed him for this office." Schmucker went on to describe the "ordinary evidences" of the inter-nal call as "undoubted piety," "at least a mediocrity of talents," and "a desire or at least an ultimate willingness to serve God in the ministry."[27] Schmucker made no effort to harmonize his views with the Lutheran confessions, but by claiming that the "regular call" consisted of an *inter-nal* and an external call, he gave vague confessional cover for an extra-confessional concept.

"American Lutherans" built on Schmucker's sparse discussion of the inner call. H. L. Dox argued for the necessity of "the internal con-viction that God requires us to preach his word" and approvingly cited the questions put to ministerial candidates in the Episcopal Church:

"Do you trust that you are inwardly moved by the Holy Ghost to take upon you the office of the ministry?" According to Dox, this conviction is the product of "the Word, the Spirit and the Providences of God."[28] If the conviction were true, said Dox, it will be clear, lasting, deep—that is, all-pervading and controlling. "The will of God" regarding a call to ministry, according to an 1860 *Evangelical Review* article, "is to be learned from the teachings of the sacred Scriptures, studied under the guidance of the Spirit, always bestowed in answer to prayer. The Divine direction will be given . . . by means of the Christian's own conscience, judgment and sanctified affections."[29] A common theme was the conviction that one could be singularly useful in the ministry compared to other vocations.[30] As the century progressed, proponents of the inner call more freely described it as a direct spiritual experience. Advocates spoke of "the movings of the Holy Spirit on the soul," "a direct inner call," "a voice in the soul," and a communication that is "immediately from God."[31]

Discussions of how one knows God's will, along with concerns raised by "direct" experience language, related to proponents' argument that the inner call was not "enthusiasm." Schmucker again set the trajectory: "This conviction [the inner call] is not at the present day produced in an immediate, extra-ordinary or miraculous manner."[32] Furthermore, ordination—which Schmucker and others equated with the external call—held accountable any claims to an inner call. Luther Alexander Gotwald combined this responsibility of the church with an insistence that the inner call was not merely a "preference," "consent," or "desire" but a "calm, rational conviction" that "comes with the force and dignity of . . . an overwhelming and ineradicable sense of duty." He encouraged psychological reflection "in the sacred retreat of the individual consciousness" on the part of the candidate.[33] Appealing to "scriptural evidence" as a "means" of the inner call was another increasingly popular method for deflecting suspicions of enthusiasm.[34] Wittenberg Theological Seminary professor D. H. Bauslin claimed the inner call mediated through Scripture *was* the "regular call."[35] In the "mediate call,"

C. A. Hay distinguished a "twofold summons by the Holy Spirit": one through God's word and the other through the church.[36] Another means, or "instrument," according to George Diehl, was "the truth," as encountered through experience.[37]

These caveats did not add much to their descriptions of the phenomenon. They never laid out any method for determining what counts as "scriptural evidence" of an inner call or for interpreting "experience." Gotwald's achievement was only to make the inner call more cerebral in late nineteenth-century terms. Moreover, the pride of place they gave to the inner call in relation to ordination strained any claim that ordination was a serious control. Some even argued that the church's role was not part of the call but only assessment and acknowledgment of a candidate's inner call, anachronistically interpreting Luther's controversy with Catholics over ordination as a battle over what body—the clergy alone or the church as a whole—had the right of "solemn acknowledgment of the inner call to this office."[38] Henry Ziegler was clear that "ordination is based on the divine internal call, which it recognizes and confirms," and where it operates apart from the inner call, it is "destitute of divine authority, and, therefore, valueless and dangerous to the true interests of the Church of Christ."[39] This was put starkly by Diehl, who argued that "the call comes from heaven but it must be recognized by the Church. By the Divine Spirit the Church is moved to ratify the work of heaven."[40] In other words, the call itself happened not through the church on earth but in some unseen realm.

Inner call theology was so dominant among "American Lutherans" that nearly all the terms and concepts relevant to ministerial call were put in service to the notion. Harkey claimed that the "appointed means" were not primarily the church structures that extend a call but personal qualifications, including "an inward abiding conviction that it is our duty to serve God in this office."[41] Supporters even used biblical examples of the external call to argue for the inner call. John Bachman described a minister as one "who when the Spirit of God addressed his heart as it did the fishermen of old 'Follow me and I will make you

fishers of men,' yields obedience to the heavenly call." This, said Bachman, is one "called and set apart."[42]

The dominant inner call theology had one outspoken "American
Lutheran" critic. In the early 1880s, Frederick Conrad publicly challenged the "prevalent theory," which he characterized in the following
way:

> A call to ministry emanates directly from God; that it is
> addressed to particular individuals; that the conviction of their
> call is impressed upon their minds in an extraordinary manner,
> through the immediate influence of the Holy Spirit; that they will
> be introduced into the ministry by the grace and providence of
> God; that few if any who have devoted themselves to other voca-
> tions and professions, were called to the ministry.[43]

Conrad charged that this view lacked scriptural support, was vague
and ambiguous, failed to explain its methods, was dangerously individ-
ualistic, and sprang from Reformed roots. He countered with what he
called the "true theory," in which "the call is not miraculous but rational, not extraordinary but ordinary, not immediate but mediate." For
all his protestations, however, Conrad still operated largely under the
assumptions of the "prevalent theory." Although he carefully avoided
endorsing the term *inner call* or any of its synonyms, Conrad insisted
that the Holy Spirit "induces [the person called] to choose the ministry" apart from the church's role, which was to help the person "form an
intelligent judgement that he is called to the ministry." Like Gotwald,
he disavowed enthusiasm by emphasizing the rational elements of this
conviction. And like Hay and Bauslin, he appealed to Scripture as the
"indirect manner" of being convinced of a call. "Such impulses, impressions and persuasions, culminating in a conviction of a call to the ministry," wrote Conrad, "can only be produced by the apprehension of
such truths contained in the Scriptures, concerning the ministry, as
constituted arguments, reasons, or motives, adapted according to the

laws of the mind, to call it forth in consciousness."[44] Conrad was a frank
critic of what he saw as enthusiastic tendencies in ministerial call, but
he still understood the call as something that happens apart from the
specific call of the congregation or larger church.

"American Lutheranism" presents the clearest correlation between
the doctrine of ministerial call and sacramental theology since the
Reformation era. As with Andreas Karlstadt and John Calvin, several
"American Lutherans" rejected baptismal regeneration and the bodily
presence of Christ in the Lord's Supper—these were among what
Schmucker saw as the "errors" of the Augsburg Confession. In other
words, "American Lutherans" consistently carried into the realm of
ministerial call the presupposition that divine things are not transmit-
ted through material things but experienced in a spiritual realm.

GENERAL COUNCIL

Leading up to the Civil War, a conservative and confessionally strict
movement developed within the General Synod. The group formed a
rival seminary in Philadelphia in 1864 and a new organizing body in 1867
called the General Council. Despite its differences with the General
Synod on the sacraments—the General Council believed in baptismal
regeneration and Christ's bodily presence in the Supper—observers at
the time did not see a substantial difference between the two Lutheran
groups on ministerial call.[45]

In 1874, General Council theologian Henry E. Jacobs wrote an influential essay on the doctrine of the ministry, with an extended treatment
of ministerial call. Jacobs's essay was in much the same spirit as Conrad's
critique. According to Jacobs, the doctrine of the word of God and the
doctrine of the call to ministry were linked. Since the ministry depends
on God's word, any defect in the doctrine of the word "will end in either
doubt and uncertainty, or positive error concerning the call." Jacobs
claimed that the orthodox theologians rejected the notion of the immediate experience of an inner call either in biblical times or in the later
church age. Such a notion, said Jacobs, sprang from a belief that Scripture

is insufficient, a view he pinned to Catholics, Quakers, and other Protestants. The result, said Jacobs, was that "the individual is turned away from the revealed word of God, to search within himself for an undefined inner call" and lacking "any test whereby a true inner call . . . may be distinguished from the vagaries of the individual's fancies."[46]

Jacobs did not dismiss the notion of the inner call. He claimed that orthodox theologians supported it as "the movement of the Holy Ghost upon the mind of the individual, in leading him through the study of the outward word of God, to the conviction that it is his duty to seek the holy office [of ministry]." This was not the call "properly speaking" but only "preparatory to the call." He refused to regard it as necessary; it may occur before or after an outward call or not at all. Where it is lacking, said Jacobs, "that outward call [through the church] itself constitutes the individual a true Christian minister." Still, Jacobs implied that the inner call was desirable, for in the case of a minister who never hears the inner call, "the Church may have made a grievous mistake in entrusting the holy office to such hands."[47]

Jacobs differed from most "American Lutheran" leaders by refusing to make the inner call necessary—much less a precondition of an external call—and by rejecting the notion that an inner call was either a separate call from or an essential part of the regular call. Most emphatically, Jacobs distanced himself from those who taught an immediate inner call. But his claim that the inner call was *never* immediate (i.e., that the immediate call of biblical times was never an inner call) subtly shifted the ground of discussion, freeing him to speak of the inner call with complete deniability regarding enthusiasm. And he sided with "American Lutherans" in treating the inner call as desirable and portraying the external word of God as means for the inner call.

General Council writers following Jacobs were often not as nuanced. Some ignored the external call altogether. According to George Hodges, "the 'call' to the ministry is the desire in a man's soul . . . to communicate the blessings of religion."[48] General Council writers often accepted the inner call as normative while stressing the importance of the external call. In his published outline on the ministry—which he claimed represented the views of General Council pioneer Charles Porterfield Krauth and conservative German theologian Christoph Ernst Luthardt—Revere Franklin Weidner of the Theological Seminary of the Evangelical Lutheran Church at Chicago spoke approvingly of an inner call. With due dismissal of enthusiasm, Weidner argued that "no man should seek the office of ministry without a well-grounded persuasion that it is God's will that he should do so." This "inner call," said Weidner, was manifest by "the arousing of desires" and in "the ordinary illumination of the Holy Spirit in the Word in answer to true self-renouncing prayer." While this inner call was crucial, said Weidner, it was not to be "confounded" with the external call of the church or to be used as a test for the external call.[49]

Others were more explicit on the necessity of the inner call. Charles Armand Miller made the external call dependent on it. Since the time of the apostles, said Miller, the church "has been investing with office men who are inwardly conscious of a call to this special work. Accordingly, the ministers in the church today have the inner call to the work of the ministry."[50] In *The Lutheran Pastor*, George H. Gerberding described the inner call as necessary and "preparatory." Taking his cue from Jacobs, Gerberding claimed that the orthodox did not reject the inner call but "wanted to put it in its proper place and relation as to the outward, official call." But Gerberding was honest enough to admit that in his view, the orthodox "did not give it sufficient prominence or attach to it the proper weight and importance." Gerberding and others claimed to be restoring a balanced view of the inner call that had been neglected in more recent decades.[51]

Some General Council writers—like many General Synod leaders—presupposed that material elements cannot convey divinity. This translated to viewing the inner call as the distinct sphere of God's activity. In *The Pastor's Guide*, Jacob Fry wrote, "The call to the ministry has three sources: It must come from God, from the church, and from a particular place or congregation." Fry equated the call "from God" with "the inward drawing of the Holy Spirit, moving and constraining the will and disposition towards the work of ministry."[52] Miller echoed this sentiment, claiming the minister is made "official" by the congregational call, "but his office depends not merely upon the call of the congregation." "His inner call to the work of the ministry," said Miller, "comes from a higher source."[53]

Through the nineteenth century, Lutherans in the Muhlenberg tradition—both the General Synod and the General Council—placed increasing emphasis on the inner call and developed progressively elaborate descriptions of the phenomenon. Some, like Conrad and Jacobs, tempered the most overtly subjective versions of the theory, but their efforts did not counteract the importance of the inner call in the equation of ministerial call and may have cleared the path to discuss it more freely without the specter of enthusiasm. These Americanized groups, however, were not the only voices in the choir of nineteenth-century Lutheranism in America.

NINETEENTH-CENTURY IMMIGRANTS

Beginning in the 1840s, European immigrants greatly bolstered the number of Lutherans in America. Although they interacted with the Lutherans of the Muhlenberg tradition in the East, these Lutherans mostly formed their own denominations in the Midwest and labored to preserve the languages and customs of the Old World. These groups also tended to have a high view of the Lutheran confessions, even as many bore a deep Pietist imprint. Their views of ministerial call illustrate this tension. Without attempting to convey the views of the myriad distinct and often intertwined denominations, we can see the general contours of thought through a few select groups.

German Groups

The Missouri Synod was birthed in controversy over the ministry. The Saxons who settled in Perry County, Missouri, in early 1839 were followers of Martin Stephan, who resisted the pressures in Germany to dilute confessional Lutheranism. Stephan's followers were as dedicated to orthodox Lutheranism as they were to his leadership. Orthodoxy would not disappoint, but Stephan's leadership would, as his financial and sexual improprieties led the group to banish him just months after the people had sworn loyalty to him as "bishop" en route to the New World. In the aftermath of Stephan's removal, the group members agonized over the legitimacy of their ministry and church, but led by C. F. W. Walther, they found in Luther and in orthodoxy their justification as a church with a valid ministry grounded in the priesthood of believers.

Missouri leaders devoted significant thought to the source of the "regular call"—first as a response to the tragedy of Stephan, then as a defense against other Lutherans' high-ministry views (ministry conferred through other ministers, ordination as a divinely ordained necessity for a valid call, the sacraments performed by nonordained or improperly called ministers as not effective). In his theses on church and ministry (1852), Walther articulated his famous "transferal theory." God originally gave the rights and duties of the ministry to the congregation, "which possesses all church power." But through the call of the congregation, God transfers the ministry to an individual who then serves in the ministerial office.[54]

The Missouri teaching had the potential to refute the inner call notion. The "regular, orderly way" of call, said early leader Theodore Brohm, is "mediately," by which he meant through the church. Brohm also noted that the problem of "enthusiasts" was not that they claimed an immediate inner call when God never granted such (the claim Henry E. Jacobs used to open space for speaking of a nonimmediate inner call) but that they claimed an immediate inner call at a time when God has not promised or commanded it.[55] The implication was that any inner call was by definition immediate and therefore should be accompanied by signs, as Luther and the orthodox argued.

Yet for all these clear differences, Missouri leaders did not directly critique the inner call. In some instances, they were simply too preoccupied with defending their doctrine of congregational call over against high-ministry views.[56] Reviews of Gerberding's and Jacobs's works passed over the authors' arguments for the inner call.[57] An 1899 editorial disparaged the inner call as a basis for rogue, shallow, and uncommitted evangelism but did not challenge the inner call as such.[58] Missouri writers would occasionally endorse the inner call. In his influential *American-Lutheran Pastoral Theology*, Walther quoted Philipp Jakob Spener to justify the attention he gave to the external call, for "the internal [call] concerns only the conscience of the one called."[59] In an installation sermon in 1878, Walther briefly elaborated on the inner call. A true pastor, said Walther, must be "inwardly called by Christ to the holy office." This entails being a true believer but also "that in his heart the desire burns to bring also to others the costly pearls which he himself has found."[60] Quoting a Baptist paper, the *Lutheran Witness* told readers in 1902 that true dedication to ministry is about a minister being "persuaded in his inmost being that it was his vocation, a veritable call from God to his soul."[61] For others, the acceptance of the inner call was implicit. C. C. Morhart advised young men not to wait for the call before even considering the office, for "the call may come while you and your parents are thinking about it, and you will be able to decide quickly."[62]

The basic, if not exuberant or detailed, acceptance of the inner call among Missouri leaders also had roots in the thought of Wilhelm Löhe. A Bavarian village pastor, Löhe was devoted to missionary work and was responsible for sending over eighty mission pastors to the United States between 1845 and 1872. Like Walther, Löhe revered the Lutheran confessions. And like Walther, Löhe endorsed the inner call without integrating it into his general theory of ministry. The inner call, wrote Löhe in his influential pastoral handbook, is often manifested by "an unconquerable love and inclination toward this office." Pointing to theologians Paul Tarnow, Johann Mayer, and Johann Fecht, Löhe equated this inner call with "the driving force of the Holy Spirit" while also warning that all the inclination in the world would not amount to

a true inner call if the person lacked personal and professional require-
ments of the office.[63]

Löhe's missionaries were also influential in the Ohio Synod. But
much more prominent was Matthias Loy. Without directly attacking
the inner call, Loy showed no sympathy for the presuppositions that
bolstered it. Loy cautioned that personal qualifications do not imply
and should not be confused with a divine call. Disregarding the possibility of a modern immediate call unless accompanied by miracles "as
proof," Loy claimed the only valid mediate call was that "given by a congregation and publicly certified."[64] Theologians in other German synods occasionally criticized the inner call directly. Anyone who looks to
the "so-called inner call" to make a pastor, wrote Adolf Hoenecke of the
Wisconsin Synod, is "going the way of the enthusiasts."[65] Such pointed
objection was rare, however, and terse. Another Wisconsin theologian,
Jacob Schaller, somewhat begrudgingly allowed that the "so-called
inner call" could refer to the "inner desire and urge to prepare oneself
for ministry" of 1 Timothy 3:1.[66]

SCANDINAVIAN GROUPS

More than their German counterparts, Scandinavian American
Lutherans embraced the inner call. But they likewise did not elaborate
on it or confuse it with a call through "means."

For the Swedish Augustana Synod, the inner call was necessary
both in a technical sense and for the minister's confidence in his call.
F. A. Johnsson insisted that a minister should proceed with certainty
if he "has the assurance that he has received the inner call of the Spirit
of God in his own heart, and the outer call of the Church of Christ."[67]
Conrad E. Lindberg's standard textbook reflected this dual commitment to an inner and an outer call. After quoting article 14 of the
Augsburg Confession, Lindberg wrote, "The inner call must be confirmed by a regular external call" through the medium of the church.[68]
Although committed to the confessions, Augustana leaders did not
feel constrained by their letter. A 1917 editorial offered standard

confessional fare about the church's right of call. But the writer could not leave it at that:

> Though it does not seem to be implied in this article, yet . . . as a necessary requisite for a proper administering of the means of grace, the one called by the Church should also have what the theologians designated as the inner call. . . . In like manner [as the prophets, apostles, and evangelists of scripture] the Church calls and sends those whom she has reason to believe are endowed with the Spirit of God and have experienced the call of the Spirit to be evangels of God to men.[69]

Like the earlier "American Lutherans," some Augustana leaders made the church's call dependent on the inner call.

Nor did Augustana leaders always project great confidence in the external call of the church. According to an 1897 editorial, ministers "will time and again, wonder whether or not their call to the ministry was really from God. This question cannot be satisfactorily answered except by retreating into the closet, in order to examine themselves and their motives before the all-seeing God."[70] A 1912 editorial pleaded for a congregational system of supporting promising young men for ministerial training by referring to this support as an "initial call." Anticipating pushback from those who argued that "God should do the calling," the writer countered, "If the voice of [God's] people should not prove to be the voice of God and be followed by an 'inner call,' the money advanced might be returned."[71] Such comments demonstrate that not only was the inner call necessary but the role of the community was uncertain.

The lack of a clear explanation of the inner call, coupled with an insistence on it, caused some problems. In the early 1880s, seminary student Constantinus Esbjorn (later, professor at Augustana College) admitted he didn't know exactly what an inner call was. Discouraged by the fact that he lacked the experience, Esbjorn feared he would have to perjure himself to satisfy a church that might want to hire him.[72]

Some apparently also thought they shouldn't pursue the ministry without the experience, even if they were otherwise inclined. To counter
this, C. J. Sodergren tried to demystify the inner call:

> Is not the *need* of ministers a "call"? Is not your love for souls,
> your own prayer for humanity, the wishes of a parent, your desire
> to be of some special use, the advice of a pastor, a sermon from
> the pulpit—is not some or all of this a voice sufficiently clear, an
> index-finger pointing in the direction you should go?[73]

Another attempt to reduce the mystery of the inner call claimed that
"the possession of the requisite *gifts* and the *love* for some special occupation constitutes a 'call' to that vocation."[74]

Those considering or preparing for ministry often reflected their
leaders. Seminary students of the Norwegian Hauge Synod, expected
to profess an inner call, commonly left before finishing their studies, pleading the pull of their inner calls.[75] The inner call theory also
meshed with the rhetoric of less traditional ministerial posts. The
spiritual biographies of deaconesses and those embarking on overseas
missions—both men and women—often included the inner call.[76]

Nineteenth-century immigrant groups were not as passionate or
detailed regarding the inner call as their Americanized fellow Lutherans. The Germans tended to be more forthright about God's voice in
the congregational call, and some explicitly rejected the inner call. But
they generally endorsed it, if only as a private matter. The Scandina-
vians typically considered it as necessary and even suggested that the
church's call depended on it, leading to descriptions emphasizing concrete influences and dispositions. As ethnic distinctions receded in the
next century, these characteristic approaches would increasingly come
into contact with one another and seek shared expression.

ERA OF CONSOLIDATION

Early in the twentieth century, Lutherans began processes of merging denominations. In three phases, these mergers were so effective that by the end of the century, two denominations claimed 95 percent of American Lutherans. In every phase, the inner call continued to have prominent advocates, although the understanding and application of it continued to evolve. With the greater bureaucratization occasioned by the mergers, the inner call "conversation" gradually moved from individual leaders' pens to denominational materials.

First Phase: 1917–60

The union of three Norwegian groups in 1917 created the Evangelical Lutheran Church (ELC), which provided the denominational home for nearly all Norwegian American Lutherans. The eastern Lutherans in the General Council, General Synod, and General Synod South merged in 1918 to form the United Lutheran Church in America (ULCA). In 1930, the mostly German heritage Joint Ohio, Texas, Iowa, and Buffalo synods formed the American Lutheran Church. Despite negotiations on matters of governance, church practice, and theology, these mergers occasioned no debate about the inner call to ministry. Leaders carried forward earlier positions, but with the merging of denominations, the subtle distinctions between them were blurred.

The extreme emphasis on the inner call of the General Synod continued in the ULCA, although shorn of indulgent rhetoric of direct spiritual experience and the once common claim that Scripture served as a "means." In a 1924 book, Carroll J. Rockey distinguished ministry from other vocations based on the "inner compulsion" and "inner call." According to Rockey, "The ministry is a vocation in a higher sense than it is a profession . . . for the man who enters it should, nay, even *must*, feel called to it." Rockey also reappropriated a Catholic term referring to the permanent sacramental gift given to a minister in ordination, claiming that the inner call was "the higher *character indelibilis* [sic] of a spirit devoted to the highest calling of God."[77]

As was evident in Rockey's language of "feeling called," the premium ULCA writers placed on the inner call did not prompt them to describe that experience in detail. In this, they departed from the earlier "American Lutherans." The vague description lent itself to strong subjectivism. According to Walton Harlowe Greever,

> The manner of [the inner] call cannot be defined. It is a matter between the individual and God . . . which no other man can judge with finality. It is sometimes based upon a particular experience which the individual may not be able to describe either accurately or adequately, or there may be no particular experience, and the conviction is present with no explanation.[78]

Far from being a liability, this subjectivism expressed the profound spirituality of the inner call, which, for Greever, connected with one's commitment to ministry. The radically personal nature of the inner call meant no one could judge it from the outside—at least not prior to that person's ministerial work. The church was to "discover the genuineness of the call," but this did not imply the church's call always coincided with God's will "or that it could claim to confirm the primary call from God."[79] According to Wilfried Tappert, a recent ULCA report erred in tethering the church's call to God's call. The church is not even the "confirmer" of the call, wrote Tappert, since God's "sending," experienced as "an inner constraint . . . is not subject to proof by those without except by the fruits of a man's ministry."[80] In other words, the only external confirmation comes after the fact. The inner call was determinative; the church's external call had no divine authority.

Scandinavian groups also continued earlier trends, taking the inner call for granted but not arguing for it or exploring its implications at length. In the Norwegian ELC, clerical biographies included having other career paths "displaced by an inner call to the ministry."[81]

ELC leaders saw the inner call as primary but operating in harmony with an external call.[82] The inner call was also part of the official 1950 ELC definition of deaconess.[83] In the Augustana Synod, A. D. Mattson claimed that "an inner call is ... essential for an effective ministry" and connected the inner call to conversion and piety.[84]

Midwestern German groups continued their lukewarm acceptance of the inner call. In the American Lutheran Church, leaders occasionally spoke of a "brother [who] has felt the call of his God for service in the holy ministry."[85] John Fritz's often-reprinted summary of Walther's *American-Lutheran Pastoral Theology* ensured that Missouri leaders continued to imbibe Walther's idea of an inner call that needs little elaboration, since it matters "only as far as the conscience of the person called is concerned."[86] New Testament scholar William F. Arndt was more explicit, defining the inner call as "the conviction that God wants me to be a minister of the Gospel" and relaying anecdotes of successful ministers who testified to the experience. The subjective nature of the inner call meant, for Arndt, that it was not sufficient—a nearly opposite position from certain ULCA writers. But Arndt assumed that in "normal" circumstances, a potential minister has an inner call so that he should reject a call from the church if he has a positive conviction that God has *not* called him. However, if a potential minister has an external call but no strong conviction for or against the ministry, he should accept the call, "trusting that the longed-for inner call will come in the course of time."[87] Arndt gave no directions on what to do if the inner call never came.

SECOND PHASE: 1960–88

The (new) American Lutheran Church (ALC), created in 1960, brought together the midwestern German groups of the old American Lutheran Church along with the Norwegian ELC, the Lutheran Free Church, and the Danish United Evangelical Lutheran Church. The Lutheran Church in America (LCA), formed in 1962, combined the larger ULCA and Augustana Synod along with smaller Danish and Finnish heritage groups. The Missouri Synod ultimately charted its own course, although all three groups cooperated and deliberated through the Lutheran Council in the United States of America. The postwar merg- ers provided channels for extending prior sentiments about ministerial call but also created confusion as multiple traditions sought expression in fewer, larger denominations.

With the mergers, discussion of the inner call increasingly appeared in denominational studies and statements. The 1964 ALC "Statement on Ordination and Clergy Roster" claimed that since faith and willingness to enter ministerial office are God's work, God as "the real ordainer, gives to the candidate what Lutheran theologians spoke of as the 'inner' call."[88] In 1976, the ALC's "Guidelines for the Calling and Sending of Clergy" spoke of ministers as those who "by reason of a call from God . . . are called and sent to that particular ministry." The external call depended on "a sense of call," which was "from God" in a way that the external call was not.[89] "A 'call,'" declared the LCA's Com- mission on the Comprehensive Study of the Doctrine of the Ministry in 1970, "is an official act of the church by which specific assignment is given to a specific person whom the church believes God has called to the ministry."[90] A 1974 study on ministry from the Lutheran Council in the United States of America referred to the "sense of God's call- ing" that may bring a resigned minister to seek ministerial office again.[91] These statements were ambiguous enough to lead an ALC ordination study committee to suggest in 1982 that the significance of "inner" and "outer" calls warranted more study.[92]

A significant driver of the studies and statements on ordination was the question of ordaining women, which both the ALC and the LCA began doing in 1970. On one level, appealing to an inner call would seem an obvious move: the church should stop denying the office to those whom *God has already called.* But inner call theology was more an unstated assumption than the explicit rationale for women's ordination. Beyond the wrangling over biblical passages, arguments for women's ordination tended to stress that the church should change with the times and that denying women ordination deprived the church of crucial services. Although female ministers testified to the experience of an inner call, some were uneasy with an emphasis on a personal sense of call.[93]

The official—if unclear—role of the inner call affected liturgical work. In 1973, a subcommittee on ordination for the Inter-Lutheran Commission on Worship (ILCW), which included the big three denominations, expressed interest in refining definitions of "internal and external call," but apparently nothing came of this. In its preparatory work, the subcommittee listed "acknowledgment of the call from the Lord" among its "elements of the rite" of ordination. Its 1977 ordination rite questioned the ordinand, "Are you persuaded that the Lord has called you . . . and are you willing to assume this office?" As Paul Nelson observes, this "question about being personally persuaded of a call from God, in advance of the call from God through the Church," was an innovation in Lutheran rites likely spurred by the subcommittee's study of the Episcopal rite.[94]

The innovation was not without its critics. Representing Wartburg Theological Seminary (ALC), Roger Jordahl "deplored" the rite's handling of ordination as "almost a private rite of passage for the ordained which is authenticated by the interior feelings of the candidate and then recognized and confirmed by the church." Jordahl was

> dismayed by the theologically questionable intensification of the personal emphasis in the rite as opposed to the objective external call of the Church. [It] presents personal feeling as the basic criterion for the validity of the call and would then be in contradiction to the fundamental Lutheran doctrine of the call.[95]

Responding for Gettysburg Seminary (LCA) to an earlier draft, Robert Jenson likewise objected. "Of what the candidate is or is not 'persuaded' is, by *Lutheran* doctrine, *at this point* wholly irrelevant," complained Jenson. "Here, only what the candidate now commits himself to, is of significance." Missouri representatives blandly called for "much less emphasis on subjective personal persuasion." Despite these concerns, the ILCW did not change the question about persuasion and willingness.[96]

These objections reveal uneasiness in some corners with the implications of inner call theology. However, the critiques left open the possibility that, if not belonging in the ordination rite, the inner call might belong in the candidacy process leading to ordination. Moreover, any impact of an anti–inner call position was blunted by the fact that these objections remained internal rather than published responses. This, along with the air of surprise in these responses, suggests that these critics were unaware of its prevalence and did not think it called for a robust theological response. This posture may have been reinforced by the fact that the *Occasional Services* of 1982, which supplanted the ILCW rite, omitted this persuasion language and emphasized God's call through the church.

THIRD PHASE: 1988–PRESENT

In the 1970s, a conflict in the Missouri Synod over biblical interpretation provided the momentum for further consolidation, leading to the formation of the Evangelical Lutheran Church in America (ELCA) in 1988. The new church combined the ALC, the LCA, and the Association of Evangelical Lutheran Churches, which was the splinter group from Missouri that pressed for the merger. Missouri continued its sparse and cautious acceptance of the inner call, while the ELCA unreservedly enshrined the concept, although it did not treat the inner call as the sole realm of God's voice in ministerial call or wall off the inner call from external scrutiny.

While reiterating its traditional position that the church's call is God's call, Missouri Synod leaders also recognized the prevalence of inner call notions. In "Theology and Practice of the Divine Call," the Commission on Theology and Church Relations insisted that "the so-called 'inner call' should be interpreted in light of [the] principle" of

1 Timothy 3:1 that "a man who aspires to pastoral office desires a good thing." This meant that the inner call "should not be confused with personal ambition" (presumably not "a good thing"). "One who thinks he has an 'inner call' to serve God as a pastor," the document admonished, "seeks to have that call affirmed and confirmed by the church."[97] On one hand, this brief statement encapsulated Missouri's discomfort with the inner call—referring to it as "so-called," putting it in scare quotes, laying responsibility for an inner call upon the individual. On the other hand, the document refrained from theologically evaluating the notion and implicitly reinforced it by suggesting that the church's call confirms it.

Key ELCA documents related to ministry amplified inner call theology. "Visions and Expectations," which articulated aspirations for the conduct of rostered leaders, stated, "The call comes to individuals from God both personally and through the church."[98] Although insisting on an inner ("personal") call, the document attributed both it and the church's external call to God. In "Together for Ministry," the 1993 report culminating five years of study, the ELCA asserted that the "regular call" of article 14 of the Augsburg Confession "presupposed" an inner call.[99] This echoed an association between the Augsburg Confession and inner call that Schmucker first proposed in the 1830s. Regional leaders followed the denomination's lead. "Those called to this particular calling," claimed my own synod, "are to feel an 'inner call' from God as well as an 'external call'" from the church. If so, then they rightly have a "regular call" of the kind to which the Augsburg Confession refers.[100] To clarify this inner call, the ELCA advised leaders involved in the candidacy and placement process to think of calling as

what happens when the rostered minister feels God stirring his/her Passions and Convictions, when he/she is maximizing their Gifts and Talents, and when he/she senses God pointing to a specific kind of ministry or context. Such discernment is a spiritual exercise.[101]

This description was perhaps an effort to make the inner call more pub-licly accountable and thus a return to the conception of the external call (which doesn't happen without such church leaders' approval) as "ratification" of the inner call.

Supporting materials for ministerial candidates reinforced these sentiments. Candidacy manuals, claiming to speak for the "Lutheran tradition," explained that "in the internal call an individual senses God's leading to consider and prepare for rostered ministry." The external call included both the input of others leading up to ordina-tion and "the call to serve in a specific setting," which confirmed the preceding internal call.[102] The widely used resource *What Shall I Say?* argued that "discernment begins and ends on one's knees, where God's calling voice may be heard and tested." Although reinforcing the notion that "the church's call is God's call," the booklet also urged readers to "explore whether you are being called" to ministerial office. The writers suggested that a spiritual director—that is, a professional who listens and asks questions in the service of spiritual growth and discernment— "will help you listen to and understand your inner self so that you can distinguish between God's voice and the other voices within you."[103] Paul Baglyos's recent *Called to Lead* made the inner call more explicit and detailed: "Lutheran Christians understand and teach that . . . the discernment of God's call . . . involves attending to both *internal* and *external* stirrings and promptings of the Holy Spirit." The internal dimension includes "the inclinations and aspirations that stir within an individual." For Baglyos, the external dimension included not the official call of the church but only the "counsel and encouragement of others" that should confirm internal stirrings.[104]

ELCA materials claimed to represent "Lutheran Christians" and "the Lutheran tradition" as they taught and required an inner call. Of course, one can only objectively state *the* Lutheran teaching regarding some-thing on which the confessions are silent as a generalization from many distinct versions of that concept. As this historical exploration has shown, Lutherans have had varying—and not always reconcilable—notions about the inner call. Some said it was part of the "regular call," while others saw it as an appendix. Some considered it necessary, while others viewed it as merely preferable. Some made it the precondition for the external call, while others left it in the realm of conscience. Some said the inner call was uniquely the voice of God, while others claimed God spoke harmoniously through both external and internal calls. Some insisted the inner call operated through "means," while others spoke of it as a direct spiritual experience. None of the major American leaders explicitly promoted the view that the inner call was sufficient by itself; some insisted that the external call, especially in the sense of ordination, checked the inner call claims, while others pointed to personal gifts, the results of ministry, or informal guidance from others as arbiters of any feelings of the inner call. In general, the most emphatic endorsers and elaborate theorizers about the inner call were those in the Muhlenberg tradition (the General Council, General Synod, ULCA) along with Scandinavian Pietists (e.g., the Augustana Synod, ELC) and their heirs in the ALC, LCA, and ELCA. German groups founded in the eighteenth century (Missouri, Wisconsin) tended to be more cautious and constrained in their endorsement of the inner call and on a few occasions rejected it directly. Despite these variations, the ELCA was not wrong to assert that Lutherans (at least American Lutherans) had developed a long tradition of teaching and promoting the concept.

As we shift the approach to the inner call in Lutheranism from historical description to theological construction, we must return not only to Luther but specifically to Luther's doctrine of vocation, within which the most credible account of Lutheran teaching on the call to ministry finds its place. This account offers clarification and corrective not just for Lutherans but for the whole church.

3 CALLINGS AND VOCATIONS

Give to the one who asks you.

—Jesus

IN THE PREFACE TO Luther's self-described "testimony and confession," the *Smalcald Articles* of 1537, he explained that the Reformation movement no longer sought approval or even understanding from the church of Rome, since "through God's grace our churches are now enlightened and supplied with the pure Word and right use of the sacraments, an understanding of the *various walks of life*, and true works."[1] For Luther, the teaching on vocation was at the core of the Reformation, along with scriptural proclamation and the sacraments.

Vocation is Luther's sleeper doctrine. Despite its importance to Luther, theologians and church leaders have not given it the same attention as many of his other ideas. The fact that the definitive work on Luther's doctrine of vocation for English audiences is a translation of Swedish scholar Gustaf Wingren's 1942 doctoral dissertation says something about the level of scholarly interest in the topic. Nevertheless, the concept has quietly remade the Western world—sometimes by a faithful application of Luther's teaching, often by a misunderstanding or distortion. The teaching emptied the monasteries, transformed the ideal of a church minister, hallowed the family, and helped invent the "Protestant work ethic," which played no small part in the rise of modern capitalism.

This is not to suggest that theologians have ignored this issue. Especially in the last few decades, interest in vocation has blossomed, and not only among Lutherans. Lutheran presentations have emphasized vocation as the place where the sinful self is progressively put to death, as the framework for faithful Christian living, and as the vital connection between faith and everyday life.[2] The crucial matter of *how* God actually calls has remained in the background, although it illuminates key features of Luther's teaching on vocation—namely, neighbors, structural positions, duties, faith, and vocational identities.

WHO'S CALLING?

Like all of Luther's core teachings, vocation begins in Scripture. I am convinced that Christians make vocation unnecessarily complicated, when it is in fact as simple as unfolding the implications of Jesus's words in Matthew 5:42: "Give to the one who asks you" (NIV). Vocation gets complicated when it searches for some other center.

A member of my congregation once asked me about this passage after I had preached on the text. "I struggle with this passage," she told me, shaking her head. "I know Jesus says to give, but sometimes I wonder if it's always the right thing to do." She went on to explain that her struggle arose out of her relationship with a member of her family who was often seeking financial help. "Do I really have to give to her every time she asks?" the parishioner asked me. "I've started to say no to her, but I don't feel good about it."

I responded by attempting to distinguish law and gospel alongside her. "These are undoubtedly hard words," I said. "And the context of this passage, Jesus's Sermon on the Mount, makes it clear that Jesus intends us to hear these as hard words. Over and again, Jesus ups the ante on what God's law asks of us. It is not my job to lighten the burden of the law by giving you some loophole in the law or excuse not to obey. The only release from the burden, from the guilt, is forgiveness."

In hindsight, I should have also clarified that some requests are not legitimate, since they do not arise out of genuine need, and that our proximities also establish priorities—in other words, if my charitable giving robs my children of food, I have not obeyed Christ's words. But both qualifications are an intensification, not relaxation, of the law. My sense is that our overcomplication of vocation comes from our collective desire to find loopholes and excuses. Unable to stand under the plain truth of God's demands, we respond to the question "What am I to do?" by appealing to all sorts of things other than the simple request of a neighbor. We talk about the abstractions, like the greatest good for the greatest number, and issues of personal identity, like desires, motives, gifts, talents, and—perhaps most disastrously—an "inner" call or a "sense" of call.

Many discussions of vocation begin with etymology (word history). "Vocation" comes from the Latin *vocare*, "to call." Hence *calling* is a reasonable English term for the concept. Of course, "vocation" has taken its own historical trajectory—conjuring hyperreligious notions, as in the case of the Catholic Church's use of the word as a technical term for priestly and monastic occupations. It also brings to mind hypersecular notions, like "vocational training" narrowed to instruction in specialized job skills. Meanwhile, "calling" has carved out a vaguely spiritual meaning indicating a sense of purpose and devotion in one's occupation. "This is not just a job"—you'll often hear passionate people say as they describe their work—"this is a calling." Or "This is my calling in life, and I would be unhappy if I didn't follow it." More theologically minded writers remind us that a vocation or a calling means *someone* is calling—more specifically, *God* is calling. Calling cannot be reduced to following your bliss or finding the thing you love to do so that you'll never have to "work" a day in your life.

As necessary as it is to insist that vocation only exists because God is the one calling, this emphasis on the divine source of it can ironically cloud the biblical purpose of it and cause us to miss the way callings work in everyday experience. In Matthew 25:31–46, Jesus vividly and with mixed metaphors describes the final judgment. The king—who is the Son of Man—"will separate people one from another as a shepherd separates the sheep from the goats." Putting the sheep at his right hand, the king will invite them to "inherit the kingdom prepared for you from the foundation of the world." His rationale? The sheep served the king when he was in need, giving him food when he was hungry and water when he was thirsty, welcoming him when he was a stranger, clothing him when he was naked, caring for him when he was sick, and visiting him when he was in prison. He will condemn the goats on his left hand precisely because they didn't feed, welcome, clothe, care for, or visit him. Although light-years separate the destinies of the sheep and the goats, they are united in their bafflement at this judgment: "When was it that we saw you hungry or thirsty or a stranger or naked or sick or in prison" and cared for you (sheep) or did not care for you (goats)? The king answered, What they have done or not done "to one of the least of these," they have done or not done to him.

This final teaching from Jesus before his death exposes the jugular vein of vocation. When another human in need calls to you, it is Christ himself who is calling.

NEIGHBORS AND CALLINGS

When considering human deeds, Luther insisted we distinguish carefully between the realm *before God* and the realm *before humans*. Before God, faith determines whether something is good or not. In the human realm, the only meaningful measure of actions is that of helpfulness to one's neighbors, which includes the care of the nonhuman creation as an indirect service to those neighbors. "Thus it is not your good work that you give alms or that you pray," said Luther, "but that you offer yourself to your neighbor and serve him, wherever he needs you and every way you can, be it with alms, prayer, work, fasting, counsel, comfort, instruction, admonition, punishment, apologizing, clothing, food, and lastly with suffering and dying for him."[3] As Gustaf Wingren put it, "Vocation is shaped solely according to the need of others."[4]

Even Jesus fulfilled his vocation by responding to the needs of those he encountered. As Einar Billing noted, in John 5, Jesus heals the sick man at the pool of Beth-zatha because "in the fact that [Jesus] had this day been brought into contact with the sick man, he saw a message from his Father."[5] This response to others' needs provides the coherence to Jesus's ministry that otherwise might seem scattershot. Why does Jesus help some and not others? Because these were the ones he *encountered*. While early in his ministry, Jesus was certain of his mission to Israel, the request of the Canaanite woman (Matt 15:21–28) pulled him more deeply into the work of his vocation. We could call these requests "callings," for this is the arena in which one *hears* God's voice, albeit through our neighbors.

Such callings often shape the relationships, positions, and offices we enter. A person who is frequently asked to listen to friends' and family members' worries and offer sound advice might enter the counseling profession, where he will hear even more callings to listen empathetically and counsel wisely. But in every case, the request as well as the office remains firmly planted in the present. As Gene Edward Veith Jr. writes, "Vocation is in the here and now."[6] This is strange for those who are conditioned to think about calling as a voice beckoning into an imagined future. At a pastor's retreat a few years ago, I began discussing with a fellow pastor this idea of vocation as existing chiefly in the present through other humans. "Take the case of fatherhood," I said. "I don't have any children, so I can't say that I'm 'called' to be a father. If I have a child, then I will know that I am called to fatherhood. If the child dies, I am no longer called to fatherhood." My conversation partner wasn't convinced. "I get what you're saying," he said politely, "but I still think I would be called to fatherhood without actually having any children at the present time."

This notion that calling exists somewhere outside present earthly encounters is deeply engrained. But it is a departure from biblical and Lutheran principles. Recognizing the highly subjective nature—and potential for self-delusion—of this common view, Catholic theologian Edward P. Hahnenberg presents a refreshingly concrete, earthy vision. "We discover our vocations in response to the world," he writes. "Mothers and fathers awaken to their calling by responding to the calls of their children. Teachers find theirs by responding to the questions of their students."[7] But even this perspective stops short of identifying our neighbors' requests with God's voice, instead treating them as sharpening stones for our tools of vocational discernment. Douglas James Schuurman's blunt proposal is better:

> You may have identified the need of higher education and gained the necessary credentials for teaching college, but being a professor is not your calling until and unless you get a concrete offer to teach at this or that college, university, or seminary. You may feel called to serve as a senator, but that is not your calling until and unless you get elected. You may think Mary is the one God is calling you to marry, but if she does not concur, then God is not calling you to marry Mary.[8]

The common future-focused view often uses pious language of following a call against one's wishes. In reality, a call that is understood as a personal sense of a future possibility leaves the one "called" in control of the narrative. I can report today that I feel called to be a missionary and two years later that I feel called to be a personal trainer. Although trusted friends might challenge or encourage these ideas, the conversation is set up in such a way that I remain the final arbiter of God's call. But as Jesus's encounter with the Canaanite woman reveals, a calling that comes directly through the neighbor is undeniable and often disrupts one's sense of personal mission. Even more unsettlingly, it also moves freely above and beyond the law. Jesus knew that his Father was at work in the need of the man at the pool, even though this work meant he would have to work on the Sabbath. We'll return to this issue of freedom later in this chapter.

But Jesus gives us more than his example. In the parable of the Good Samaritan, Jesus teaches how service to the neighbor is the essence of vocation. Though Luther carried over a medieval allegorical inter-pretation that identified the Samaritan as Christ and the injured man as sinful humanity, he also broke the mold by emphasizing the vocational encounter with one's neighbor when he preached on this passage. "We will find [Christ] close to home," said Luther, "in the person of our wife, child, servant, master, and civil magistrate. We will find him in our neighbor's house, on the street corners, and in the marketplace. These are the places we should be doing whatever we can out of friendship, love and duty."[9]

Interestingly, Catholic liberation theology uses the Good Samari-tan story to argue that one must not only "care for those who are close. It is also a demand to love those who are distant—or rather, to go over, *to draw close*, to become a neighbor to those who suffer."[10] While *going* to those who suffer to offer care is praiseworthy, Luther directs us to what is right in front of us. "Are we to look for our neighbor in Rome?" Luther jabbed his German audience. "Don't we have enough neighbors right around us, our wife, children, and other poor people?"[11] In the parable of the Good Samaritan, the Samaritan and the other characters who do not help the injured man *are* on the move. But they are all on the move in their regular lives and routines. None of them is intentionally seeking out the suffering. They come upon the opportunity to be a neighbor to the suffering man precisely because their earthly routines put them in proximity to the sufferer.

This proximity is the mediator of vocation. The actual call of the needy neighbor will be the difference between "call and commandment" that some writers agonize over. The call makes the commandment con-crete. The call incarnates the commandment. While the commandment says "Honor your father and mother," the call is your father saying

"Take out the trash." While the commandment says "Love your neighbor," the call is the encounter with the beaten and stripped man on the road to Jericho. This is why Jesus told the story of the Good Samaritan in response to the question, Who is my neighbor? Many well-meaning discussions of Luther's doctrine of vocation rightly emphasize serving the neighbor but also veer into the Calvinistic notion of influencing culture through vocation. This notion risks making vocation abstract and diffuse rather than the concrete, pinpointed direct personal service in Luther's understanding.

ORDERS, STATIONS, AND OFFICES

Of course, most of our interactions do not occur with strangers on the street. In any given moment, our neighbors are more likely to be people with whom we have strong bonds through family, work, church, and friendship. In that sense, our encounters usually don't seem random or chance. Vocation—which is to say, God's will—is embedded in these relationships. For all of us, these vocation relationships begin in the child-parent relationship. This is why in the *Large Catechism* Luther called the fourth commandment the "first and greatest commandment" of those dealing with our neighbors. Close behind is the sixth commandment, for the husband-wife relationship is the context for bringing forth children. But more than that, spouses have their distinct relationship, which Luther described as "the person nearest"—that is, the neighborest neighbor! It doesn't get any closer than "one flesh and blood." Marriage gives a fundamental vocation with the potential for unfolding additional vocations in the context of a family.

Our structured relationships and social positions are deeply woven into vocation. In Luther's mind, these relationships and positions fall into three categories, or "orders": church, household, and government. Church entails everything related to speaking God's words, especially the gospel. Household includes what we could call occupations, since this work is grounded in providing for one's family. And government, at heart, is an extension of the family made necessary by human sin. This leaves, really, just two categories: those relationships and positions that deal with earthly welfare and those that deal with faith—said another way, those that deal with our lives in relation to other humans and those that deal in relation to God. This overlaps somewhat with the distinction between law and gospel, but we should not be too rigid about this. After all, the church must also use "law," not only in preaching, but also in structuring its work. And within families, God calls parents to be gospel preachers—more on that later in this book.

Although one can, using reason, surmise from nature the existence of these orders, Luther also insisted that *only* these three orders are explicitly instituted by God—that is, commanded and blessed in Scripture. For instance, the church was born in God's words regarding the trees of the garden (Gen 2:16–17), and the household began with God supplying the woman as a helper for the man (Gen 2:18).[12] The classic scriptural passage sanctioning government is Romans 13:1: "Let every person be subject to the governing authorities; for there is no authority except from God, and those authorities that exist have been instituted by God." These orders by themselves are quite broad, so Luther often used the term *station* or *estate* to address more particular dimensions within them. Even more specifically, within these stations are precise offices, like mother, mayor, or preacher. For instance, a mother (office) lives in marriage (station) within the household (order). Here, "offices" most closely aligns with what I call "vocations"—that is, well-defined positions or relationships. Luther was not always exact with these terms, but the main point is clear: God has carefully ordered the basic relationships and social positions of human experience. Any way of life that does not fit in these categories—like prostitution or monasticism—is rebellion against God's will.

Through orders, stations, and offices, God maintains the earthly structure and helps creation flourish. All our work, said Luther, "whether in the fields, in the garden, in the city, in the house, in war, or in government," is the means by which "He wants to give his gifts." Creation is always the site of God's activity, and humans in their vocations are "masks of God."[13] All legitimate vocations are holy because through them God cares for his creation. Neither marriage nor the office of ministry needs the added grace of a "sacrament." Like the sun, moon, and stars praising God by providing light (Ps 148:3), humans do holy work simply by caring for creation in their own creaturely ways. As Marc Kolden writes, Luther's "most basic assumption" regarding vocation "is that the world is God's good creation, not only in terms of its original coming into being but especially in terms of God's ongoing creative work in upholding and directing all that is and in constantly doing new things."[14] God himself supplies us with food, but he does this from seed sown and harvested by a farmer, shipped by a driver, placed in the store by a stocker, and sold by a clerk. Manna does not fall from heaven; it comes to me through the work of dozens of human hands. Either way, God is the one supplying. This is one reason Luther often advised that people should remain in their vocations. He feared that if everyone hopped fences for greener grass, the basic maintenance of creation would be threatened. No doubt, the static implications of this view rub us the wrong way. We prioritize change, promotion, and social mobility, not "remaining." But as Oswald Bayer points out, we cannot escape the basic creaturely needs that can only be met in certain, unchanging ways. The orders of creation simply describe God's means of meeting these needs. Bayer calls this "the spiritual significance of all worldly things."[15]

To be sure, not all created things are spiritually significant in the same way. When a particular promise of forgiveness is combined with created elements of bread, water, and wine, God brings us into his eternal kingdom. Orders, stations, and offices, however, have nothing to do with your own salvation—although in the case of preachers, God may use you in your office to bring someone else to salvation. This is the other reason Luther insisted people should remain in their vocations; like Paul (1 Cor 7:17–20), he wanted to assure people that salvation is found in *all* vocations. In a culture that viewed monasticism and the priesthood as more certain routes to salvation, this was a freeing message.

WHAT TO DO?

The orders, stations, and offices are all gifts from God. They channel God's care to creation, especially my neighbor. But more than that, they relieve me of the burden of constantly wondering how best to care for creation. My stations in life almost always answer that question before I need to ask. As Luther said,

> If according to God's Word and command you live in your station with your husband, wife, child, neighbor, or friend, you can see God's intention in these things; and you can come to the conclusion that they please Him, since this is not your own dream, but His Word and command, which never deludes or deceives us.[16]

In other words, we hear God's call through life with neighbors. And we know it is God's call because the stations in which we hear the call have God's "Word and command." The callings can be explicit, as when a coworker literally asks for help with a project or when a teacher calls on the school janitor to help clean a spill in the cafeteria. But they can also be implicit, as when my professional job responsibilities entail collaboration with colleagues or when the janitor makes his rounds and cleans up any spills along his path. This is the dance between "callings" and "vocations." Just as requests from neighbors may lead me progressively into a particular type of work, so my office or occupation shapes the callings I hear. Mothers hear their babies crying for milk. Judges hear plaintiffs asking for justice. Grocery clerks hear customers asking for goods. "Any individual who wants to be pious," said Luther, "will have enough genuine good works to do in his own station, and he will not have to go looking for anything special."[17]

Vocations also provide the tools and methods with which to serve our neighbors. Parents have all the carrots, sticks, and behavior modeling that go into raising children. Rulers have all the laws, policies, and purse strings available for just governing. All that is left for us is to walk in the good works "God prepared beforehand" (Eph 2:10). God sends clear messages of what we are to do even through the inanimate objects of our vocations:

> If you are a manual laborer, you find that the Bible has been put in your workshop, into your hand, into your heart. It teaches and preaches how you should treat your neighbor. Just look at your tools—at your needle or thimble, your beer barrel, your goods, your scales or yardstick or measure—and you will read this statement inscribed on them. Everywhere you look, it stares at you. Nothing that you handle every day is so tiny that it does not continually tell you this, if you will only listen. Indeed, there is no shortage of preaching. You have as many preachers as you have transactions, goods, tools, and other equipment in your house and home. All this is continually crying out to you: "Friend, use me in your relations with your neighbor just as you would want your neighbor to use his property in his relations with you."[18]

Vocation is not mysterious. Rather, as Schuurman puts it, "the numerous and regular obligations that attend our varied routines and roles are expressions of what God wants us to do in our particular locations, always with a view to serving our neighbor and serving God through our neighbor."[19]

Because serving our neighbor is the beginning and end of vocation, we can be scandalously uninterested in questions of intention or motivation. God will, of course, judge the heart, but that is in the realm *before God*, not *before humans*. Perhaps the clearest example of this is in Luther's 1527 advice about whether it is proper for a Christian to flee from the plague. In all vocations, we have duties and responsibilities to others, said Luther. This does not change in an emergency; in fact, responsibilities often become more acute. Preachers must minister. Mayors must rule and protect. Fathers and mothers must protect their children. And this extends beyond the most obvious connections. For example, relatives should step in for children if their parents are gone. "In fact," said Luther, "no one may flee from his neighbor unless there is someone to take his place in waiting upon and nursing the sick."[20] A biblical view of vocation requires us to resurrect the much-maligned concept of duty. Popular writer Parker Palmer, for instance, connects duty (using terms like *standards, expectations, oughts,* and *voice of moral demand*) with a sense of inevitable failure and therefore guilt placed on us by external voices. This leads him to discard duty as a way of speaking about vocation and instead focus on vocation as a "gift" that "comes from a voice 'in here.'"[21] But such a view fails to recognize all that duty accomplishes for the neighbor. Duty pulls the newborn's mother out of bed for a two-o'clock-in-the-morning feeding. Duty brings the teenager safely home at curfew. Duty drags me to the courthouse for jury *duty,* when I have much I would rather be doing.

In his advice concerning the plague, Luther made vocation both more binding and more freeing. For while everyone has a duty to help the needy neighbor, everyone is also free where there is no need. Luther used the example of a neighbor's house on fire: "Love requires that I run there and help put out the fire." But, he continued, "if there are enough other people there to extinguish the flames, I may either go home or stay."[22] You can almost hear Luther adding, "If your help isn't needed, feel free to leave and enjoy a beer at the tavern." Luther's counsel contrasted starkly with the spiritual advice common in his day. Since the Roman Church taught that good works were necessary for salvation, it tutored people always to seek them out—not for the neighbor's sake but for one's own benefit. In the scenario of the neighbor's fire with plenty of helpers already on the scene, the logical extension would be to force oneself into the emergency. But if such action does not actually help the neighbor, it is a false piety.

FAITH AND VOCATION

This raises the question of how faith relates to vocation. On one hand, vocation is fundamentally a matter of creation—what theologians call a "first article" concern (i.e., the first article of the Apostles' Creed). God uses humans to serve and provide for one another, often without their understanding of God's works. Because of the "divine foundations and orders" that shape our vocations, we can say that "even the godless have much about them that is holy."[23] Luther learned fully what Paul says in Romans 2:14: even those "who do not possess the law, do instinctively what the law requires." God even uses sinful actions and impulses for his good purposes. As Luther explained of human sexuality, "The Lord fulfills his blessing; and people are begotten, though in sin and with sin."[24] For although good fruits come naturally from good trees—that is, Christians—God's work is also accomplished through donkeys and pharaohs. Vocation does not begin, as some claim, "with freedom from the law" experienced through forgiveness.[25] For Christians as well as non-Christians, all life situations and experiences involve vocation, since all of life is lived in relation to others. Even when no official role is involved—whether a legal role like an employee or a biological role like a parent—one is always related to others as a neighbor. The obligations of an office can be radically different from those of a neighbor to a neighbor. An officer of the court is obligated to imprison people. As a neighbor, the same man is forbidden to do so. But being a neighbor is still a vocation—that is, a sphere in which one person can make requests of or claims upon another—just as the Good Samaritan discovered! Luther railed against monasticism, and often offered his positive view of vocation alongside criticism of monasticism, because he saw the life of the monk or nun as fundamentally an attempt to rid oneself of neighbors. "To do the will of God," said Luther, "does not mean to put on cowls or gray coats and run away from human society into the monastery. It is not written [in God's word] that we should do these things, but . . . that we should . . . be found in a calling that has a word of God."[26]

Recognizing that God cares for creation through unbelievers as well as Christians, Wingren and others suggest that unbelievers have divine *offices* or *stations*, while Christians have *vocations*.[27] But this distinction shifts the center of gravity away from God and toward the human. Rather, to have a station means also to have a vocation. In Luther's words, "How is it possible that you are not called? You have always been in some state or station; you have always been a husband or wife, or boy or girl, or servant."[28] Just as the determinative factor in the Lord's Supper is Christ's presence, not whether you believe it, the determinative factor of vocation is that God calls, not whether the hearer recognizes the voice as divine. Vocation does not depend on the faith or psychology of the individual.

On the other hand, faith will make a difference in how we experience our vocations. Christians may not be the only ones who find joy in their vocations. (I suspect those who opine about the "random, meaningless" worlds in which nonbelievers are "trapped" doth protest too much.[29]) But faith alone knows what is happening in our vocations. And so Luther spoke of the "power and drive" that come with knowing that God's will permeates one's vocation.[30] Every request—momentous or mundane—is an invitation to participate in God's relentless care for creation. Christians know the purpose of human encounters. People often illustrate such "purpose" with the parable of the bricklayers. The architect asks them, "What are you doing?" One replies, "I am laying bricks to feed my family." Another replies, "I'm building a cathedral." According to the parable, the one building the cathedral truly has a sense of purpose. But the insight of vocation is that the divine purpose encompasses both perspectives. Feeding my family and building a cathedral are equally taking part in God's fatherly, divine goodness.

FREEDOM OF A CHRISTIAN

Faith also leads us into what Einar Billing praised as the "spontaneity and naivete" of Luther's understanding of vocation.[31] Although critics of Luther fault him for his static view of occupations and social roles, his view of vocation has a joyful spontaneity deep in its core. We never know fully what requests may come to us; we should expect the unexpected. While our defined roles make many of our vocational tasks routine, we never know when a Canaanite woman may come begging for her daughter's healing. And since all requests are God's voice so long as they spring from legitimate needs, answering these calls is not optional. Those seeking to live a biblical view of vocation can expect to have their plans disrupted.

This spontaneity is related to a blissful naivete. One aspect of this naivete is the Occam's Razor of judging ethical behavior simply on the grounds of the neighbor's good. Luther's suggestion that preachers can decide among themselves who should stay and who should go during a plague relied, after all, on the perhaps naive notion that *all* the preachers were willing to stay (or return). But again, this is not so much a concern about intentions as a concern that the neighbor's needs are met. If the preachers could not come to an agreement about who would stay, or if they were not all willing to stay, they would all, ironically, be duty bound to stay, to ensure suffering people had ministers.

Another aspect of vocation's delightful naivete is the way we can think about the many requests that come to us. Living in vocations means encountering more voices of God than one can answer. God may even seem to be contradicting God when two honest requests are made of me that are mutually exclusive. Even with our expected and routine tasks, Luther recognized that we never meet all the demands:

> Are you a husband, and you think you have not enough to do in that sphere to govern your wife, children, domestics and property so that all may be obedient to God and you do no one any wrong? Yea, even if you had five heads and ten hands, even then you would be too weak for your task.[32]

Vocation frees us from the myth of the "one right choice." Rather, right answers abound, so long as your choice of action does good for the neighbor. This is true also for the decisions that seem more significant in our lives, like the choice of a spouse, college major, or occupation. Too often, we imagine that one path is correct (or better) and that God leaves us to our devices to discern that path. Sometimes this search turns us into amateur ethicists, weighing relative goods of imagined outcomes. Sometimes it turns us into aspiring mystics, trying to find a sign of God's will in the heavens or in our hearts. In both cases, the actual neighbor before us is demoted to a secondary consideration.

As a teenager, I joined a Pentecostal church. In Pentecostal circles, one hears folks often speaking about how God speaks to them, leading them toward or away from something. I learned that, especially when making big decisions, you should pray and expect God to indicate God's will in some way. Sometimes people testified to hearing a voice or getting a clear (if inaudible) message; sometimes they said they discerned God's will by a feeling of peace connected with a decision. When I was in ninth grade, I signed up for baseball at my school. I hadn't played since elementary school, and I was looking for a way to connect with some of my school friends. A few weeks into practices, I started to get a guilty feeling. I hadn't prayed about the decision to play baseball. For a ninth grader, it *was* a big decision: lots of practices added on to my already full schedule with school, church, and a part-time job. The feeling of guilt grew over a few days, until I lost any sense of enjoyment lacing up my cleats and taking the field. So I quit. And I felt bad about the whole experience—guilty for not "seeking God's will" as I had been taught, embarrassed for bailing on my new teammates, disappointed in myself for not committing.

Although this might be an extreme scenario, the presuppositions at play are not uncommon. Even writers attempting to present Luther's perspective slip into the subjective language of a "sense of calling" and allude to the "mistakes and sins we make as we prayerfully discern our callings."[33] To be sure, mistakes and sins will occur *in* our callings. But the combination of "discernment" language with the threat of sin in that discernment can reinforce the notion that there is a "right" decision when it comes to vocation and responses in our vocations. Not only does this invite us to rely on our works to be "right" before God, but it is an unrealistic simplification of ethical decision-making. The thought-provoking television show *The Good Place* (2016–20) summarizes the conundrums of ethics in the modern world:

> Life now is so complicated.... These days, just buying a tomato at a grocery store means you are unwittingly supporting toxic pesticides, exploiting labor, contributing to global warming. Humans think that they are making one choice, but they are actually making dozens of choices they don't know they are making![34]

The myth of the "one right choice" is an unnecessary burden. God asks us not to divine the mystery of his will but to do good in the opportunities before us. As Wingren wrote, good works "pour in on man from the outside, through the very movement of life."[35] Let God sort out how he can make mutually exclusive requests, ask more than you can give, or harmonize your interests with opportunities to serve your neighbors.

This is not to say that vocation lowers the bar of God's demands; in fact, it brings us face-to-face with our failures and inadequacies. As Veith writes, "The [Lutheran] doctrine of vocation is utterly realistic, accounting for problems, sins, and confusions that beset each and every vocation."[36] You have always left some good undone. At the end of every day, God called to you—through a spouse, a coworker, a friend, a stranger—and you did not answer. You must repent for that. You may misjudge a request and end up enabling—and thereby participating in—someone's sin. You must repent for that. Even if you could somehow manage to perfectly meet every legitimate request, you can't rely on that to calm your conscience, for God condemns you for looking for assurance of salvation somewhere other than Christ. You must repent for that.

For this reason, the ultimate freedom in vocation is nothing other than the freedom of the gospel—that is, forgiveness. Only with the assurance of absolution can we move freely in our vocations, led by our neighbors' calls rather than self-interest—whether of the blatant greedy kind or the sneaky works righteousness variety.[37] As Steven D. Paulson writes, "Justified by faith on account of Christ means you suddenly have new *time* that is not taken up in hide-and-seek religion and you have new *space* or ways of actually helping others that come through your 'calling' in life."[38] I'll give to the one who asks, knowing that my gift will fall short, that it will make me complicit in some sinful system, and that I'll be tempted to think I'm righteous for giving. Such perils are only overcome if my salvation is completely removed from the equation of service to my neighbor. In this way, vocation blossoms most fully. Alluding to Luther's famous counsel to "sin boldly," Kathryn A. Kleinhans writes, "Since the Christian is simultaneously saint and sinner, sin is inevitable in this life; but since Christ died for 'true' sinners rather than 'fictitious sinners,' the Christian need not be paralyzed by the fear of making the wrong choice or doing the wrong thing."[39] Forgiveness frees us from concern about how God—and by extension, other human beings and society—judges our deeds and choices. All that remains, then, are the claims our neighbors make on us.

The comfort of forgiveness is matched with the encouragement that in faith, our deeds are actually good. As Romans 14:23 says, "Whatever does not proceed from faith is sin." But in faith, our good works are, finally, good (although still mixed with sin). They are good not because faith adds some missing ingredient to the good works recipe but because they are done freely, for the neighbor, without coercion of God's law—that is to say, they are done by the Holy Spirit in us. In Luther's language, such works make God smile: "When a father goes ahead and washes diapers or performs some other mean task for his child . . . God with all his angels is smiling—not because the father is washing diapers, but because he is doing so in Christian faith."[40] Although non-Christians often do what is required in their vocations, this does not entitle them to God's thanks, let alone his smile. As

Jesus says in Luke 17:9, "Do you thank the slave for doing what was commanded?"

The works that pour forth from believers in their vocations will often be like new wine in old wineskins. God's law cannot fully account for them. After all, the law does not prescribe specific behaviors for every situation. In James Arne Nestingen's words, "The law runs behind on short legs."[41] The same is true for the orders, stations, and offices we inhabit, since these are expressions of God's law. But rather than solving this problem by putting a fence around the law like the Pharisees, constricting human behavior to have greater assurance of not violating the law, the gospel opens us to courses that are unwritten and unforeseen. "The gospel leaves us to our own counsel," said Luther, "that we may decide and act in matters as we would."[42] Christians are, rather, bound to the open-ended law of love:

> Above these three institutions and orders is the common order
> of Christian love, in which one serves not only the three orders,
> but also serves every needy person in general with all kinds of
> benevolent deeds, such as feeding the hungry, giving drink to the
> thirsty, forgiving enemies, praying for all men on earth, suffering
> all kinds of evil on earth, etc.[43]

The Christian in vocation does not live by a list of rules and is even free to make new laws. This is terrifying for those wishing to be justified in the black-and-white prescriptions of the law, but it makes perfect sense to those who through baptism, forgiveness, and the work of the Holy Spirit "walk in newness of life" (Rom 6:4).

VOCATION AS A CROSS

The comfort, encouragement, and freedom Christians enjoy do not shield them from the pain involved in their vocations. Work is cursed with trouble and toil; this is true for Christians and non-Christians. But Christians experience suffering as a cross, meaning suffering is part of

God's redemption, since suffering leads to hope, and we are saved in hope (Rom 5:3–4; 8:24). The medieval monks, with their self-inflicted austerity, understood this. Where they went wrong was in assuming that suffering needed to be sought. Rather, as Wingren wrote, "The cross is not to be chosen by us; it is laid upon us by God, [that is,] the cross comes to us uninvoked in our vocation."[44] Christians will experience additional evils, since they have a powerful enemy. The devil wants not only to wreck our faith but to get us to forsake our callings through trials, temptations, or even feelings of "dislike and disgust."[45] In our day, we could add that Satan's tactics include a lack of feelings of "fulfillment" that we demand from our vocations. Furthermore, the Christian feels suffering as a contradiction of God's promise, like Abraham did when God asked him to sacrifice Isaac or as Jesus did on the cross.

For unbelievers, suffering is the unfortunate way of the world, to be avoided when possible. The world, said Luther, "cannot stand the idea that in a divine station it should serve other people with nothing but care, toil, and trouble, and get nothing as a reward for this but ingratitude, contempt, and other malicious treatment."[46] But Christians recognize that suffering is required in the service of our neighbors. We do not serve only to the last point we can stand the inconvenience, but we "suffer and die" for the good of our spouses, children, employees and employers, governments, and enemies.[47] This is the "living sacrifice," Paul urges upon believers (Rom 12:1). We need only recall Luther's advice about conduct during the plague to know what this looks like in practice. For this reason, the promise of angelic protection (Ps 91:11–12) is specifically for those "engaged in our calling and in the performance of our duty, by a command from God or from men who have a legitimate right to call upon us."[48] Satan's use of this scriptural passage to tempt Jesus to throw himself from the temple was an unholy testing of God because Jesus's vocation was to die not leaping from the temple but nailed on the cross for our sins. Precisely because of this promise of protection in our vocations, however, Christians joyfully risk with their time, resources, and lives.

WHERE AM I IN THE EQUATION?

In his book *Awakening Vocation*, Edward P. Hahnenberg lays out two traditional approaches to vocation. One approach, which stems from John Calvin, suggests that God has predetermined each person's ideal callings. As Hahnenberg argues—and I also contend in this chapter—this approach can lead a person to a precarious quest to discover God's will for them. People look in many places for insight. Calvin himself stressed how one's talents, abilities, and gifts aid in the discernment process. Today, we continue to talk about talents, but we also increasingly stress the psychological dimension. Christians have gravitated toward the language of sensing or feeling a call. The non-Christian world has its own terminology, usually involving the concept of "passion." A person's sources of enjoyment, motivation, excitement, and a sense of purpose are the clues to what they should pursue in work, romance, and their social life. Early in the story, the characters in Disney's animated film *Soul* (2020) see things this way. Prior to birth, each soul is assigned a distinct personality profile, but the soul is only ready to be born when it has discovered its "spark," which could be anything—photography, basketball, baking, painting, firefighting, gymnastics. (Without spoiling the film, I should note that the truth about how souls get born turns out to be more nuanced.) Christians, of course, also use this language, often infusing a vague altruism with Frederick Buechner's famous dictum "The place God calls you to is the place where your deep gladness and the world's deep hunger meet."

As convincing as this sounds to our modern ears, the "passion" narrative is problematic theologically, since terms like *passion* or *gladness* are easily misused as pretentious cover for what we simply *want* to do. Even straight-talking conversations on vocation easily devolve into what Hahnenberg calls "efforts at identity enhancement,"[49] and vocation becomes, effectively, a series of choices. The process of choosing a major in college is the great modern image of this. The student literally reads a list of areas of study, each representing a vocational arena, and is expected to make a choice that will set a life trajectory. Despite pious language of God as the "caller," if the guiding force is really a pursuit of passion, one has left the biblical view of vocation behind.

Even without mention of God, the common model of "finding your passion" is misleading and potentially harmful. As researchers have begun to argue, the search for a stable, inherent personal "inner reality" is misguided. Rather, we are like jazz musicians, constantly improvising to ourselves the melody of our identities based on the chord changes of life experiences. The idea that passions are "things found fully formed" within us is unrealistic, since "it's through a process of investment and development that you develop an abiding passion in a field." If we believe that passions live in our DNA, we also are more prone to give up on difficult tasks—even when they are in our area of self-described passion—since the common narrative suggests that a true passion comes with endless stores of motivation. If we run out of steam, we figure, it must not be our "true" passion.[50] Without realizing it, we stifle our own potential through the pursuit of passions.

The other approach to vocation, stemming from Luther, emphasizes human freedom and simply lays out the boundaries within which Christians may faithfully serve. According to Hahnenberg, this approach has its own problems, for it "risks washing out the particularity of the person."[51] But this is only true if we fail to recognize Luther's insight that God's voice is the call of the neighbor. God reveals his vocational plan for me (yes, me) by speaking directly to me every day through my neighbors. What could be more personal, individual, and particular than the requests I hear from my spouse, my child, my coworkers, my friends? My vocational identity is not the thing within me that propels me into the future. Rather, except in the rare occasion of a prophet's calling (Jer 1:5), my individuality in vocation comes from outside me, and I discover it after the fact. My vocation as a father began with the positive pregnancy test, and this vocation is unique to me because of who my child and wife are. By the requests they make of me as a father and the environment they help create as I perform my vocation, they form me into a father unlike any other.

This view of vocation requires radical faith in God's providence—not as a fuzzy divine decree before creation but as experienced and unfolding throughout one's life. What may seem like chance or random encounters are in fact the neighbors whom God wishes one to serve, just as the Father directed Jesus to heal the sick man at Beth-zatha and the daughter of the Canaanite woman. Over time, these encounters shape one, not as a person in oneself, but as a servant in relation to others. For as Luther said, a Christian lives not in himself but in Christ through faith and in his neighbor through love. This radical replacement of our "selves" means we don't have power over our bodies or other resources. Paul taught that "the wife does not have authority over her own body, but the husband does; likewise the husband does not have authority over his own body, but the wife does" (1 Cor 7:4). This is not a license for spouses to abuse each other but a reflection on marriage as the core neighbor relationship. Nothing is ours; all things belong to the neighbor. In the height of the Covid-19 pandemic, I often heard people whom I know to be Christian rationalize lax use of protective measures (like masks) by saying, "If it's my time to die, I'm OK with that." The sentiment might have a stoic appeal, but it fails the test of vocation. While you might be OK with your death, your neighbor who relies on you is not. This is why Luther considered those who refused to protect themselves from the plague to be suicides—with the damnation that implied.

Living by faith in God's providence and by love in our neighbors, we can let go of the quest, summarized in one college student's words, "to answer the question of what kind of future God has planned for me."[52] Instead, we can focus on what kind of present God has given us. Apart from my interactions with neighbors, I can never get a handle on who I am in any of my callings. And I will never fully grasp my vocational identities on this side of eternal life, since the calls keep coming. Yet I must trust that God knows what wife and child to give me, what job opportunities to provide me with, what neighbors to bring before me so that the person who emerges from these vocational encounters is *me* and no one else. In these encounters God is the potter, molding us, his clay, as he pleases. The task remains to apply this view of callings and vocations specifically to the work of gospel ministry.

4 CALL TO THE OFFICE OF MINISTRY

> The office of preaching, as an office, is clearly one
> office among others. . . . Nevertheless through this
> particular vocation God carries out something dis-
> tinctive and totally different from all other vocations.
>
> —Gustaf Wingren, *Luther on Vocation*

IN TERMS OF HOW God's call relates to the office of ministry, Luther
treated the office of ministry as any other vocation. The previous chapter laid out this basic theology:

- God calls through neighbors.
- Vocation exists for neighbors' benefit.
- Vocation is structured through orders, stations, and offices,
  which make apparent one's obligations.
- Christians experience the freedom of action in vocation, the joy
  of performing good works in faith, forgiveness that opens time
  and space for serving, and mundane and demonic suffering that
  leads to hope.
- One's vocational identity is forged in the furnace of one's offices
  and neighbors' requests.

In one sense, then, all that should be left to do is apply those principles to the ministerial office—that is, to describe the kinds of neighbors who call someone to this office, the requests (callings) that typify this vocation, the temptations and trials that beset it, and the types of vocational identity it forms. Yet like Jeremiah, we must uproot as well as plant, pull down as well as build. As outlined in earlier chapters, the Lutheran teaching on the call to the ministerial office became unmoored from the basic theology of vocation by the adoption of the notion of an inner call. This concept has become so popular that any account of ministerial call that ignores it seems negligent. The first task, then, is to evaluate the theological and practical implications of the inner call notion. Then we can discuss what Luther called a "true call" to the office of ministry, analyze the functions of the inner call in light of Luther and the confessions, and provide suggestions for today's church.

THEOLOGICALLY EVALUATING THE INNER CALL

In 2003, John A. Molstad Jr., president of the Evangelical Lutheran Synod, wrote that "very sparingly, Lutherans have used the expression 'inner call' to mean the God-placed desire (1 Tim 3:1) to serve in the public ministry."[1] As we have seen in previous chapters, Lutherans have spoken about the "inner call" more than sparingly, and its meaning has not always been limited to "the God-placed desire to serve in the public ministry." The Lutheran embrace of the inner call is strange for several reasons. First, the notion was invented as a crucial element of monastic theology (the disdain for "the world") that Lutherans rejected. Second, the frequent claim that Scripture serves as a "means" for the inner call runs against the grain of the traditional Lutheran approach to Scripture. Third, not only was Luther vehemently opposed to the notion, as we saw in the first chapter, but it fails to align with Luther's core conception of Christian living.

Monastic Origins

When Andreas Karlstadt became the first Protestant leader to endorse the notion of an inner call, he was not recovering some clear proposition from Scripture, but neither was he inventing a new concept. According to Catholic theologian Edward P. Hahnenberg, "It was the monk who bequeathed to the church the notion of the inner call."[2] This notion, which emerged in the fourth century, entailed a forceful logic. The call to monastic life *had* to be inner, spiritual, nonmaterial because the external world was precisely the harmful and deceitful thing the monk was called *to flee*. How could that which was deceitful lead to truth? In the thirteenth century, Thomas Aquinas "introduced a distinction between God's external call (coming through Scripture and the example of Jesus) and God's internal call (the movement of grace [on the soul])."[3] Aquinas taught that Jesus's command to the rich young man (Matt 19:21) to sell his property, give its proceeds to the poor, and follow him is an external call to the monastic life and "is to be understood as given to all." But when an internal call, "which is to be preferred to any external speech," accompanies this external call, the command becomes even more obligatory, such that one ought not to even consult with humans before obeying the call.[4]

Later Protestants—including Lutherans—carried on two elements of Aquinas's teaching. First, Scripture serves as a call to a spiritual vocation. Second, the internal call is more forceful than the external. Of course, Protestants differed in important ways. Rejecting monasticism, they transferred this discussion of call to the office of ministry. Although Catholics later also applied the inner call to the priesthood, Karlstadt's campaign may have been the very first application of the inner call to the ministerial office. Protestants also did not view the call through Scripture as applying to everyone. This would have contradicted their argument that God calls people to all legitimate stations and offices.

SCRIPTURE AS MEANS

Lutheran advocates of the inner call recognized that they could be charged with "enthusiasm" if they did not carefully explain that the inner call came "through means." They often (especially in the nineteenth century) argued that Scripture was one of the regular tools God used to call individuals to the ministerial office. Luther, however, saw things differently. For Luther, the "mediate call . . . is a call that is made by a medium, which is *man*."[5] The medium is not experience, truth, or even Scripture but *other people*. The Scripture-as-means claim has the appearance of good Protestant commitment to the Bible, but it finds no support in traditional Lutheran standards of scriptural interpretation or application. Fully evaluating the Scripture-as-means notion would involve more arguments than would fit in this chapter, but I offer two core contentions.

First, the Scripture-as-means notion fails to justify the way it applies Scripture to individuals selectively. Since not everyone is called to ministerial office, the claim that Scripture can be a means for the call might seem like an extension of the notion that although the *meaning* of Scripture is unchanging and universal, the *application* of Scripture is context-specific. Certainly, we ought to apply Scripture differently to individuals where *Scripture itself* warrants that difference. Fathers, husbands, wives, children, masters, and servants have distinct responsibilities (Col 3:18–4:1; Eph 5:22–6:9), and God has specific directives for tax collectors and soldiers (Luke 3:12–14). God's word offers threats to the proud and encouragement to the weak. Likewise, Scripture ought to be used to teach, admonish, warn, and comfort (2 Tim 3:16; Rom 15:4), but not indiscriminately. An important part of pastoral work is to discern the contexts and conditions of other people so the appropriate scriptural words can be applied.[6] Even words of direct command do not always apply to Christians—for instance, the rituals prescribed for the Israelites. The issue, Luther said, is always "whether it fits us."[7] The common thread is that these different applications are grounded in the distinctions that already exist and are apparent to others; we are not

free to apply Scriptures that have no connection to one's evident context or condition. The Scripture-as-means theory, however, proposes to
apply Scripture differently to different people based solely on personal
internal experience that is inaccessible to others—namely, whether one
senses a call through Scripture or not. It is a method of Scripture application that is hopelessly circular.

The second problem—which cannot be totally separated from the
first—is that the Scripture-as-means approach scuttles the Lutheran
insight on law and gospel. According to Luther and the confessions,
God's word always functions as law or gospel, or both. When one
"senses" a call to ministry through the words of Scripture, is it law or
gospel? Unless one can show how such a call amounts to "the proclamation of the grace of God" expressed most sharply in the forgiveness of
sins, it is not, properly speaking, gospel.[8] One could perhaps argue that
this call is law in the sense that it lays a divine demand upon a person. This
would require, of course, the recognition that such words always accuse
and terrify the conscience, as law is bound to do. Understandably, no
Lutheran proponents of the Scripture-as-means idea regard Scripture
as perfectly clear or sufficient to establish this demand; rather, it is but
one ingredient in the inner call stew, along with "sanctified affections,"
conscience, qualifications, judgment, and the persistence of the impulse.
Luther, however, argued that the only thing necessary for Scripture's
internal clarity—that is, for the same clear words to accomplish God's
will *in me*—is the Holy Spirit. This belief in Scripture's clarity, like the
law-gospel framework itself, refers to the effect of God's word upon its
audience. For this reason, Steven D. Paulson argues that "the proper
context for the distinction of . . . law and gospel is preaching, not interpretation or hermeneutics regarding a 'text.'"[9] Unable to commit to clear
Scripture that acts unambiguously on human hearts as law or gospel,
advocates of the Scripture-as-means theory place themselves outside
the bounds of classic Lutheran approaches to Scripture.

LUTHER'S CRITIQUE

As we saw in chapter 1, barring a miraculous witness proving one has an immediate call from God or the emergency wherein a Christian finds himself without other Christians, Luther had only contempt for the notion of an inner call to ministry. But commentators have often not acknowledged Luther's clear position. To discredit Luther, Catholic polemicists in the seventeenth century accused him of claiming an immediate call for his own ministry.[10] Today, scholars occasionally claim that Luther advocated for the inner call. One commentary on the Augsburg Confession baselessly asserts that Luther taught "some inner and spiritual event connected with the external call."[11] Eager to claim Luther, several recent evangelical writers make unsupported claims that Luther held a doctrine of the inner call like that of current evangelicalism.[12] Others fail to explain Luther's qualifications on the inner call, leaving the impression that Luther regarded the inner call as common or necessary.[13] For a casual investigator, the overall impression can be quite misleading.

Still, we must apply Luther's basic opposition to the inner call carefully. Luther's invective against the inner call involved several of his concerns, most of which are virtually nonissues for Lutheranism today. Luther knew of no preacher who appealed to an inner call and who at the same time submitted to external authority—at least not in a way that satisfied Luther.[14] When Luther encountered those claiming an inner call, he encountered Zwickau prophets, Thomas Müntzer, Karlstadt, and Anabaptists. These and others like them who, as Luther saw it, preached in secret and sowed dissension among the laity were "the devil's messengers," since they would not be subject to authorities God had established and therefore did not teach publicly and transparently. "The Holy Spirit does not come with stealth," said Luther. "He descends in full view from heaven. The serpents glide in unnoticed. The doves fly. You can be sure that this secretiveness is characteristic of the devil."[15] Luther's experience taught him that to appeal to an inner call was inseparable from "storm[ing] against

God's accustomed order."[16] The interest in divine order paralleled Luther's concern for correct teaching. By the time Luther read Karlstadt's tracts on images and the Eucharist, Luther was convinced that his former colleague had reintroduced works righteousness, pushing Christ out the back door. For Luther, Karlstadt's appeal to an inner call was part and parcel with his distortion of the sacrament, wherein Karlstad "undertakes to make everything spiritual which God has made bodily."[17] Furthermore, Luther saw in Karlstadt the motive of greed, for Karlstadt was able to claim double income from Wittenberg and Orlamünde.[18] Justly or not, Luther associated the claim of an inner call with disregard for order, unsound doctrine, and immorality.

Admittedly, Lutherans today have structures in place that (in theory, at least) rule out potential ministers guilty of insubordination, heresy, or depravity. Denominational candidacy committees and congregational call committees review ministers who are presumed to submit to order, preach God's word purely, and live uprightly. We can, therefore, disentangle the concerns about the inner call from these other issues in a way Luther didn't. But that doesn't mean we should disregard Luther's critique. Morality, order, and doctrine were side issues for Luther when it came to the call to ministerial office. Luther's intuitive suspicion about the inner call flowed from his understanding of the radically external nature of Christian life. Most have simply not grasped just how serious Luther was when he said that the Christian lives not in himself but in Christ by faith and in neighbor by love. This "ecstatic" notion (in the sense of living outside one's self) is "Luther's contribution to Christian spirituality."[19]

The inner call notion, in contrast, rests on an assumption that the Christian can "live in himself." In this supposed sphere, the Christian stands unrelated to the neighbor—and therefore "hears" inwardly. Ministers and potential ministers may embrace the inner call notion because, like the secular concept of "finding your passion," it hints that truly called ministers will have endless intrinsic motivation for a task.

In this way, rather than biblical or Lutheran concepts of vocation, it sounds more like Gramma Tala speaking to Moana:[20]

> You are your father's daughter
> Stubbornness and pride
> Mind what he says but remember
> You may hear a voice inside
> And if the voice starts to whisper
> To follow the farthest star
> Moana, that voice inside is
> Who you are.

With its focus on "who you are," the inner call concept functions like the Catholic *character indelebilis*—that is, with regard to ordination as a sacrament, a priest receives a permanent personal spiritual mark—although *character indelebilis* arguably offers a more stable ground for affirming a "sense" of call. Twentieth-century Lutherans such as Carroll J. Rockey even used the term *character indelebilis* to describe the inner call (see chapter 2). Both concepts attach ministry to individuals by an unseen, spiritual movement rather than locating it in the life of the church on earth. Both the inner call and *character indelebilis* place ultimate significance on the person in ministry, whereas for Luther, ministers "are to be chosen by the church only for the sake of the office."[21] For the ministry to be sacramental "in reference to the ministry of the Word," as the *Apology of the Augsburg Confession* states, means it is sacramental not in terms of the individual being ordained or according to some churchly structure but for God's people as a whole.[22] Luther could therefore conceive of a person who moves in and out of the office of ministry depending on a community's needs and a person's present capacity:

> When he is no longer able to preach and serve, or if he no longer wants to do so, he once more becomes a part of the common

multitude of Christians. His office is conveyed to someone else, and he becomes a Christian like any other.[23]

Some charge that this view denigrates ministry as something that is merely "functional." But such a criticism is only warranted if the church, in calling its ministers, disregards its God-given duty to call qualified individuals or if ministers, in carrying out their ministries, forget that service is, in Timothy J. Wengert's words, "dying for the other."[24]

PRACTICALLY EVALUATING THE INNER CALL

In addition to its theological problems, the inner call concept raises practical concerns. In particular, the church has not recognized the possible implications of the inner call concept on ministers' certainty and commitment in their vocation. Furthermore, the church has not been clear-eyed about the interplay between an internal and an external call. In an era of hand-wringing about ministers' well-being, these issues are potentially significant.

Certainty

In a 2017 study, the Barna Group found that more than one-third of pastors are at high or medium risk of burnout, and three-quarters know at least one fellow pastor whose ministry ended due to burnout or stress.[25] Although burnout and defection from the ministry may not be the epidemic some internet Chicken Littles claim, clergy well-being is a growing concern. About half of all pastors report that their jobs are more than they can handle and that the pastorate is frequently overwhelming.[26] Pastors leaving ministry may not be tragic per se, but to the extent that pastors leave under duress or their effectiveness is impaired by burnout, this is a problem.

Defined as "a loss of effectiveness and confidence in work, associated with decreased energy, enthusiasm, and confidence," burnout is a complicated phenomenon with many contributing factors and potential mitigators.[27] One facet that researchers have begun looking into is the relationship between burnout and calling. One study found that pastors who reported a greater sense of work as a calling or greater affirmation of their calling, however, reported less burnout and more life satisfaction.[28] The fact that research uses "sense of calling" terminology indicates the hold the inner call notion has.[29] Since burnout is a psychological phenomenon, we certainly can't speak meaningfully about it without reference to *internal* categories. But we can also understand the language of "sense" of calling differently—that is, *certainty* that God calls from outside ourselves through neighbors. The distinction could be put this way: the location of *call* is not the same as the location of the *sense* of call in the same way that the location of the computer I am currently typing on is not in my mind (much less my soul or spirit), but my sense of the computer *is* in my mind. Although the research does not make this distinction, I propose that the Lutheran perspective, locating call in the neighbor, is a more stable source of a "sense" of call that may likewise combat burnout. Those factors often associated with the inner call—passion, desire, or firm will—are inherently unstable. Even the presumably more stable traditional indicators of the inner call—qualifications and gifts—can be perilously subjective, as the burnout phenomenon has shown to cause people to question their abilities.

To be sure, perceiving my computer in front of me is more straightforward than recognizing a needy neighbor as God's call. This means that Christians need to be convinced that the neighbor's call is God's call. I hope the previous chapter contributed to this effort. Ultimately, sensing the neighbor's request as a divine call is an article of faith. But as with the physical elements of the sacraments, we can more easily grasp God's activity when it is in created things. Faith that God directs our callings in this way provides a certainty that repels burnout, as Luther recognized:

This faith creates rest, contentment, peace and banishes the tired spirit. But where it does not exist, and man judges according to his own feelings, thoughts, and experiences, behold, there is a weary and discontented spirit; for he experiences only the evil of his own lot and not that of his neighbor; on the other hand, he does not see his own good side nor the bad side of this neighbor. Hence there follows out of this feeling weariness, dislike, worry, and labor, and he becomes impatient and dissatisfied with God.[30]

A recent conversation with a fellow pastor brought this home to me. At the time of our conversation, she was two years into her first pastoral position. She explained to me and a group of fellow early career pastors that her congregation had offered her a limited-term call rather than following the "normal rule of permanency" for calls. She interpreted this "probationary" agreement partly as a sign of the congregation's nervousness about having a female pastor. She confessed to us that the church's noncommittal posture, along with interpersonal problems with parishioners, was causing her to question whether she was called to the ministry, suggesting it might be easier to leave the ministry and find a job in retail.

"I am sorry," I said to her. "Shame on your congregation for not issuing you a proper call. Of course you are questioning your call, because in one sense, the church hasn't actually *called* you." But I recognized that simply excoriating the church would not offer her any hope. So I pressed on, telling her that not having a permanent call from a congregation is regrettable, but it doesn't mean she was not called. "Calling," I said, "is present in the request of others for your pastoral service." A more robust (open-ended) call arguably provides the security necessary for the sometimes unpopular pastoral work, but in this unfortunate circumstance, her limited-term contract ought to fill the same role—this group of believers has requested her preaching and teaching. That is a call, plain and simple. She thanked me for the encouraging words.

COMMITMENT

A pastor's lack of certainty in his or her calling may be related to a lack of commitment. Although ministers should not be doormats aiding and abetting parishioners' sinful abuse, a Lutheran view of calling requires that we set our faces (Luke 9:51) toward our work despite obstacles and resistance. As we are convinced that God calls us by the plain display of a neighbor in need, the trials and sufferings that we incur in the realm of our vocations (very carefully and precisely defined) can never be the legitimate cause of leaving the ministry. As we saw in the discussion of vocation broadly in the last chapter, vocation involves suffering. Such difficulties are not merely the inevitable collateral damage of vocation; in fact, they are God's further work upon us, continually crucifying our sinful selves and training us to trust him. Furthermore, the work itself is at risk if those who are called do not persist in the face of danger. Recall how Luther responded to the vocational issues involved in dealing with the plague. Even at great personal risk, preachers, he said, are "obliged to stay," since "in time of death one is especially in need of the ministry." Reminding his readers that the good shepherd lays down his life for the sheep (John 10:11), Luther said preachers ought to hear this word as a commandment "to stay and remain where there is a peril of death."[31]

I fear, however, that churches and seminaries are not painting this full picture of vocation for ministers and potential ministers. In a meeting with fellow pastors during the Covid-19 pandemic, I heard one colleague expressing his distress that his congregation had determined to continue to worship in person—a position he worried put his health at risk. As he asked for prayers, another pastor chimed in. "Remember, we are not called to be martyrs," she exclaimed. "This was not part of the vows in the ordination service."

She was technically correct. Nowhere in our liturgy for ordination are pastors singled out for martyrdom (although Jesus's words about the good shepherd laying down his life for the sheep are a suggested Gospel reading). But such a blanket rejection of suffering in vocation—if that was how she meant it—is far from the biblical view of ministry or of vocation more generally. I don't want to suggest that pastors are called to recklessness in the name of conducting business as usual. The decision of the mode of meeting during a pandemic requires careful deliberation. Pastors and congregations must consider physical well-being alongside spiritual well-being. But pastors *are* called to martyrdom if responding to the legitimate needs of the neighbor brings them in harm's way. In fact, even apart from the public office of ministry, "we are duty bound," said Luther, "to suffer death, if need be, that we might bring a single soul to God."[32] I cannot say that this pastor's dismissal of vocational suffering was connected to any particular theory of ministerial call, but I worry that the common view of calling as something ultimately private and inward allows just enough wiggle room to shirk responsibility in moments of trial. But when our starting point is that the voice of a needy neighbor is the voice of God, we have far fewer escape hatches. The church needs pastors who are certain of their calling and willing to suffer and die to carry it out.

RELATION TO THE EXTERNAL CALL

Today, Lutherans generally understand the inner call to be necessary but not sufficient in itself as a calling. No one may enter the office of ministry based *only* on an inner call. But we should honestly consider how the necessity of an inner call plays out in the process of forming and placing a minister. Where an inner call is made necessary, it becomes the ruler and master of the external call. Describing the inner call as "presupposed" has often, in practice, meant not that it is taken for granted in ministerial candidates but that it is a prerequisite in need of verification.[33] If approval for ordination rests on a satisfactory articulation of one's inner call, the external call functionally becomes but the servant of the inner call.

A TRUE CALL

Luther looked to Jesus as the model preacher. The reformer told his Wittenberg congregation when preaching on the Sermon on the Mount, "These are the three things which every good preacher should do: First, he takes his place; second, he opens his mouth and says something; third, he knows when to stop." The minister "taking his place" is not just about ascending the pulpit, according to Luther. Rather, this is the minister's presentation of himself as "one who comes with a call and not on his own, one to whom it is a matter of duty and obedience."[34] As Luther understood it, assurance of God's call to the office of ministry is crucial for both the pastor and his flock.

Perhaps Luther's most poignant remarks on the nature of the call to ministerial office appear in a 1525 sermon on Matthew 7:15–23, Jesus's warning to beware of false prophets. After addressing the immediate (inner) call that "comes from heaven" and must be accompanied by miraculous signs to be valid, Luther spoke of "the other call," which

> is the request of the congregation or of the government to go. This is a call of love. . . . For you and I owe it to each other to love our neighbor as ourselves. For when he needs my assistance and asks for it, I am in duty bound to come to his help, for the Word of God commands that I should serve my neighbor. Then this call does not require a miracle, because they themselves desire it, and the Word of God urges me thereto. This is to be in demand, to be called and to be driven.[35]

The most important thing to note about Luther's understanding of ministerial call is how it fits precisely into his broader vision of vocation. While chapter 1 situated Luther's position on ministerial call in the context of his understanding of God's presence and activity in the material world, here we zero in on its relation to Luther's understanding of vocation. "The pastor's calling," wrote Werner Elert in his magisterial summary of Lutheran teaching, "is exactly analogous to worldly callings," even if it is the highest office in Christendom.[36] As the influential 1529 church order of Johannes Bugenhagen (Luther's pastor at Wittenberg) put it, ministers "receive before the congregation the spiritual calling according to which they may be called 'ordained to the ministry of the Spirit.'" Not only did this stress the public and external nature of ministerial calling ("before the congregation"), but it established the similarity of ministerial call to other callings. Bugenhagen continued, "Thus another received a worldly calling, which is nevertheless God's, in that he is called to be a burgomaster, a civil servant, etc."[37]

Although the significance of gospel ministry is such that God may take direct control of the call "from heaven" to ensure it, this is the exception. As with all vocations, the normal course is mundane: when people need you and request your help, and you are able to serve, this is God's call. Those who hear this call are duty bound to respond, which is an act of love. This seems to be a jagged pill for those invested in reserving even the smallest space for a pure, immaterial realm in which to sense God's "stirrings" or insisting that the call to ministry must come with the abstract conviction that one can be more useful in ministry than in any other vocation. Richard Wilbur has it right in his poem "Love Calls Us to the Things of This World." The poet describes a state between sleep and waking in which one might imagine that laundry hanging on a line is something heavenly—angels, even. This reverie betrays our desire for what is "bodiless and simple," searching for a place where "nobody seems to be," since *somebodies* are inconvenient and demanding. Yet the dream is not sustainable; by the merciless heat of the sun, the dreamer is pulled into physical reality: laundry is laundry, clothing all kinds, "thieves" as well as "lovers" and even "nuns." Just so, our neighbors call to us—like the heat of the sun, pulling us out of our pleasant heavenly trance—to recognize that love calls us not *from* but *to* "the things of this world."[38]

Centered on the need of the neighbor, Luther's notion of ministerial call was never much concerned with the minister's desire—pious or otherwise—to serve. In fact, he mentioned "desire to preach" rather in the context of not wanting many to have this desire, since that could lead to confusion. Luther claimed he was called to become a doctor of Scripture against his will; he was "forced and driven" to the work "out of pure obedience."[39] When he spoke of regularly called ministers, he spoke of "the true office, into which no one forces his way (even though his devotion urge him) without being called by others having the authority."[40] What mattered, instead, was God's will, for God "drives and urges those whom he wants, so that in short they must come whether they will or not."[41] God drives and urges people into the ministry through the call of those who are in need. Luther reasoned plainly that "if he is wanted, it is a true call."[42] Although Luther at times emphasized the personal qualifications of ministers, the importance of the call from the community remained paramount. The called minister serves the congregation with the certainty of God's word "though he be a rascal."[43]

The call of love means that a minister is bound. Even Luther confessed to wanting out of the ministry, "but the poor souls won't let me stop."[44] The point is not that ministers ought to be unhappy in their work but that the ministerial office—like vocation generally—is grounded in objective duty rather than subjective states like desire. The communal call that puts a minister in office also constrains that minister to serve, since "the ministry is not mine; it belongs to all the others."[45] True ministers, then, "will not desert their office through discouragement at the difficulties and ingratitude of men."[46] A telling example of this is in Luther's own decision to return to Wittenberg after nearly a year of protective seclusion following his condemnation at the Diet of Worms in 1521. Although he faced the possibilities of arrest and execution, Luther defended his decision to return, against the elector's will, by first pointing to his call and the "urgent begging and pleading" of the Wittenberg congregation members for their pastor's presence. Because of this unmistakable external call, Luther pleaded to the elector that he was compelled by "Christian love, trust, and obedience" to fulfill his duties.[47]

Although neighbors' requests are the driving force of vocation, order is crucial. Not all those hearing calls from neighbors to minister should themselves serve. For this reason, the *office* of ministry is central to Lutheran views of ministerial call. Ministry work is not the sole preserve of those in the office, as the next chapter will explore. But the order inherent in the office is crucial for two reasons. First, it is distinctly public. When Philip Melanchthon explained the "regular call" of the Augsburg Confession with a reference to Titus 1:5 ("Put in order what remained to be done, and . . . appoint elders in every town"), he was not merely stating his preference for episcopal ordination but clarifying that the Lutheran churches understood this as entirely an external public process, mediated through human authorities beyond the potential minister.[48] This means, most importantly, that people in need of ministry know whom they can turn to, certain that the person in the office is publicly accountable and duty bound to serve. Second, the office functions, much like other publicly recognized and accountable vocations, as a stable job description. Quite apart from the individuals who are or may be in the office, the church can be certain of what it calls ministers to do, and ministers can be certain of what they are called to do. This is even more certain because the office of ministry is a divine institution—the job description was written by God.

WHAT GOD ACCOMPLISHES IN THE OFFICE OF MINISTRY

All Christians recognize that the office of ministry is different from other vocations in some fundamental way and that this difference is somehow "spiritual" in the sense of relating to something outside the present material realm. Despite the problems with the inner call notion, many American Lutherans have attempted to identify part of this spiritual difference in the way God calls people to this office. The true difference, however, is not in how God calls ministers but in what God accomplishes through them. By magnifying the true uniqueness of the office of ministry, we can hope that the inner call notion may be less appealing.

Many—including Lutherans themselves—have claimed that Lutheranism has a deficient or half-formed doctrine of the ministry, with the result that "there is no consensus among Lutherans on the understanding of the ministry."[49] Some say Lutherans inherited this problem from the reformers themselves, since the Lutheran confessions say little about ministry, suggesting that ministry is "incidental and secondary to the real controversy" Martin Luther and his colleagues engaged in.[50] But forms and structures need to be distinguished from origin and purpose. Although Lutheranism has had great variety—and therefore often confusion—in forms and structures of ministry, the origin and purpose of ministry are clear to anyone who wishes to find them in Luther and the confessions.

In fact, Luther's movement fostered and depended on a distinct doctrine of the ministry, differentiated from the hierarchical and sacramental views of the Roman Church on one hand and the anarchical opinions of enthusiasts on the other. This theology of ministry flows from the core concern of justification (election). According to article 5 of the Augsburg Confession, the ministry is God's means of creating justifying faith, of electing sinners for salvation. God's election is the source and root of the ministry.[51] This—and only this—is where the office of ministry differs from all other vocations. As Luther said,

> A preacher occupies a public station and is an official person; correctly considered, such a person performs the greatest works, signs, and wonders that take place on earth. Through his office, through the Word and the Sacrament that he administers to you, he brings you to faith, rescues you from the power of the devil and from eternal death, and leads you to eternal life in heaven. This far surpasses all outward signs and wonders.[52]

Every other calling ultimately serves to maintain this old world; the ministry alone brings the new world. No other office has as its sole purpose to speak for God a word that "rescue[s] us from the power of darkness and transfer[s] us into the kingdom of his beloved Son" (Col 1:13). Since faith brings one into God's kingdom, which is the new creation (2 Cor 5:17), and since faith comes by hearing (Rom 10:17), we should say with Luther that "the Kingdom of Christ is contained in the public oral office of preaching."[53]

Insofar as it is an attempt (perhaps unconsciously) to spiritualize or aggrandize the office of ministry, the inner call notion stems from a failure of confidence in the proper "end" of ministry: faith. The ministry is "the highest calling" not because it arrives with some inner communication from God or because it adds a spiritual *something* to certain individuals but because God speaks through it ("Whoever listens to you listens to me"; Luke 10:16), and through that speaking, God justifies the ungodly by faith.

Flagging confidence in what the ministry accomplishes is tied to confusion about the nature of ministry itself. Although the Augsburg Confession is intentionally narrow in defining the office of ministry as preaching and teaching the gospel (which also includes judging doctrine) and administering the sacraments (which also includes excluding open and unrepentant sinners), pastors wind up taking responsibility for many other things under the pretense of the ministerial office. As Timothy J. Wengert writes in his study of ministerial office, "Pastors think their calling is to do everything except exercise the public office of ministry."[54] Of course, pastors are not inventing responsibilities on their own. They face pressures from parishioners to serve in roles more akin to social workers, party planners, community organizers, or CEOs. Their denominations urge them to attend to myriad demands with uncertain connections to article 5 of the Augsburg Confession. According to the Constitution of the Evangelical Lutheran Church in America (ELCA), ministers of word and sacrament are responsible not only for preaching, administering the sacraments, conducting public worship, and providing pastoral care but also for being spokespersons for the denomination and speaking "publicly to the world in solidarity with the poor and oppressed."[55] The Lutheran Church–Missouri Synod (LCMS) "Supplement to the Diploma of Vocation" (letter of call) identifies duties such as "assist[ing] the congregation in adopting administrative policies and procedures that will help it carry out the mission of a Christian congregation."[56]

Perhaps such obfuscation through addition is inevitable, since, as Gerhard O. Forde wrote, "there is a kind of conspiracy, sometimes unwitting and unconscious but sometimes quite conscious, to keep the mystery [of God's election] hidden away."[57] Sinful human nature does not want God to elect some to salvation purely by grace, much less in such a low and seemingly random way as through the mouth and hands of another sinful human. Related to this, the ministry is perhaps the only vocation whose results can never be measured, since faith is decidedly not sight (2 Cor 5:7; Heb 11:1). This is surely a maddening prospect in our data-driven era! And so we instinctively tack on functions and objectives—even "outward signs and wonders"—to the office to demonstrate its effect.

Certainly, local circumstances might necessitate additional bullet points in a pastor's job description. Too often, however, such extra responsibilities (which may in some cases legitimately serve the central tasks) are laid on the minister without distinguishing between them and the duties that *constitute* the office—proclaiming God's word and administering the sacraments. Where these nonspiritual functions swamp the ministerial office, the spirituality of the inner call appears especially attractive as compensation. But if the church can restore its confidence in what God promises to accomplish through the office of ministry and clearly articulate the nature of the office, I suspect it will not be quite so tempted to distinguish the office through other mechanisms, like the inner call.

IMPLICATIONS AND SUGGESTIONS

If the inner call notion is as problematic as I'm suggesting, churches—starting with Lutherans—should begin approaching the recruitment, training, and placement of ministers differently. This process begins with an honest evaluation of the language of "inner call." However the term is qualified or muddled by language like "stirrings and promptings," it suggests that God speaks to individuals in some realm apart from the natural senses and that this speech beckons hearers to the office of ministry.[58] But if the inner call is indeed *God* calling, then it should be attended by signs, as Luther advised. This would attest to the public nature of the call. Some might respond that, in the normal course, the church's external call attends the internal call, thus publicly attesting the call. But then one wonders why the inner call is necessary to begin with, since the external call is sufficient and we are certain that it is God's voice, as Luther and the confessions make clear. On the other hand, if the inner call really just refers to a psychological process of becoming convinced that one desires the office, has good motives, and so on, we should stop using the term *call* to speak about it. Here no one is "calling" anyone else to do anything; it is a conversation in a person's head.

Even if the preceding pages are somewhat convincing, churches may be reluctant to address the issue, partly because the inner call concept is so entrenched and partly because it seems quite useful in many of the church's endeavors. Seminary websites and publications beckon potential recruits to "follow their calling" and attend retreats for those "discerning a call to ministry." Appealing to a sense of call seems to be a strong recruitment tool. And it also commonly appears in fundraising efforts. Potential donors read testimonials of students who "from a very young age . . . felt a calling to the church," who "are able to enter seminary after feeling a strong calling from God."[59] In a time of declining enrollment and financial hardship in seminaries, institutions will not likely be inclined to discard communication strategies that seem successful. Beyond seminary, the inner call notion plays a role in how pastors and their denominational partners approach the process of placement in a ministry setting. When seeking a first position or subsequent post, she must reflect in writing on her "sense of call."[60] As I suggested above, "sense of call" could be carefully defined to refer to the certainty that God is calling precisely through neighbors. But nothing in the literature indicates this is the way seminaries and denominational leaders are using the phrase. So even without using the term *inner call*, this rhetoric trades on the concept, for it speaks of a "call" that is sensed, discerned, or felt apart from the actual requests of neighbors.

The results of a nonscientific survey of ELCA and LCMS staff responsible for ministerial candidacy illuminate and somewhat complicate this.[61] The survey asked respondents to rate the importance of *inner call, sense of call, duty, personal characteristics*, and *professional characteristics* on a scale of 1 (not important at all) to 5 (very important) in their conversations with ministerial candidates (see figure 1). These ratings were then averaged. For ELCA staff (*n* = 29), *personal characteristics* had the strongest importance, followed closely by *professional characteristics* and *sense of call* (tied) and *inner call*. *Duty* was rated the least important. For LCMS staff (*n* = 12), *professional characteristics* was rated most important, followed, in order, by *personal characteristics*, *sense of call*, and *duty*. Rated least important was *inner call*.

These results point to the important role of the inner call in both the ELCA and the LCMS but with clear differences in emphasis. Although the inner call was not the strongest in importance, individual respondents in both denominations rated it "very important," and only one in each denomination rated it "not important at all." Based on averages, *duty* was least important for ELCA respondents and second-least important for LCMS respondents. But the survey found crucial differences. Compared to ELCA respondents, LCMS participants were overall less interested in both *inner call* and *sense of call*. Not only did those in the ELCA show a stronger average rating of *inner call*; all but one of their ratings were between 3 and 5 on the scale, while LCMS respondents' ratings on

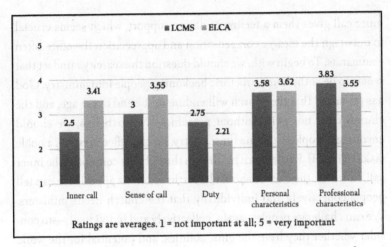

Fig. 1. Factors in church leaders' conversations with ministerial candidates

inner call were more evenly split. In general, the results align with the emphasis given to the inner call in each of these denominations. As seen in chapter 2, the ELCA has heartily embraced the inner call language, while the LCMS in recent years has more guardedly employed the concept. Regardless, to excise the inner call or sense of call language, or to increase the importance of duty, denominational staff and machinery would have to adjust not just the language on forms but the very structure of formal and informal conversations around job placement.

Certain corners of the church have lived with this conceptual framework for so long that it might be difficult to imagine an alternative. Beyond suggesting that the minister should have endless wells of motivation and serving as a spiritual distinguishing mark for the ministry, as I explored above, the inner call concept intends to meet several other psychological and practical needs involved in the church's work of recruiting, training, and placing ministers. I propose that if we identify these needs, we can suggest other ways of addressing them.

First, the concept is partly aimed at encouraging people to consider pursuing the ministerial office as a career. Priming people to hear an inner call gives them a feeling of divine support, which seems crucial to outweigh the meager compensation and appreciation the office often commands. To begin with, we should question the scarcity mindset that seems to lie at the core of rhetoric beckoning people into ministry. God has promised that the church will endure to the end of the age, and the church does not exist without preaching. Nevertheless, we should encourage people to pursue the ministry, for the office presents a noble task (1 Tim 3:1). Rather than trading on the dubious concept of the inner call, however, the church should be forthright in its appeal. We can tell people collectively and individually that the church needs ministers. We can challenge people—again, collectively and individually—to consider whether they have the gifts, abilities, and potential for the work. For people we know well who exhibit these qualities, the word can be a direct and personal encouragement. Throughout history, people have profitably sought occupations precisely because these two things meet: a general need exists, and they have the potential to helpfully serve. This practical approach would probably mean that a greater proportion of ministers were raised up from within their congregations to pursue the office of ministry.

Second, the inner call seems to be a way of addressing motives—an issue that stretches all the way back to Andreas Karlstadt. Nobody wants people entering the office for an easy paycheck or to satisfy their own desire for attention, exert arbitrary control over others, or take advantage of others in moments of vulnerability. Rather than using the inner call as a spiritualized code for this, we can address these issues of motive frankly. After all, we don't want people entering nonclergy jobs for warped reasons either, but we don't require them to articulate their "sense of call" at every turn. As best as possible, churches should investigate the objective evidence of motives. Most denominations and churches already do this through psychological screenings, reference checks, and—yes—placement paperwork. If we sense a need for language to substitute for "inner call," we would be better off speaking of things like "conviction" and "intention." Potential ministers can articulate their conviction that they have the potential to serve and their intention to be committed and faithful servants of others through the office of ministry. These concepts are not necessarily any more stable or reliable than a sense of an inner call, but they are more honest. This language suggests a similar process of intentional and forthright contextual self-examination without implying that God is somehow speaking silently to people.

Relatedly, the language of the inner call may also be an attempt to add gravity to the process of applying for ministry, as it reminds those who must report the experience that they are claiming something about God—even if indirectly. To say one senses something about God's purpose seems weightier, I suppose, than to report only on one's own purposes. Perhaps one is less likely to deal dishonestly when God is invoked in this way. But as Christians, we ought to put more stock in Jesus's command to "let your word be 'Yes, Yes' or 'No, No'" (Matt 5:37).

The inner call is a somewhat elastic phenomenon that potentially serves many functions. What I've laid out here does not exhaust the topic. But I hope it helps the church be more critical about how the concept functions and open to adjusting its language and practices.

5 PRIESTHOOD OF BELIEVERS

Comfort one another with these words.

—1 Thessalonians 4:18 (KJV)

ONE DAY A FEW years ago, I was meeting with a middle-aged couple in preparation for their wedding, which I was to officiate. First things first, I wanted to get to know them better, as they were both relatively new members of our congregation. I knew that the bride had children from a previous relationship. While she and her husband-to-be were faithful churchgoers, her teenage daughters rarely attended. I started with a simple question: "How old are your girls?" After she answered, she went on to answer the question she suspected might lie behind my question. "I know you don't see them in church much," she said earnestly. "I never wanted to force religion on them. I want them to decide on their own if they want to be Christian. That way, it's more meaningful."

This is a sentiment that many pastors have heard before and that many more pastors suspect influences the child-rearing practices of parents in their churches. It is a problem, but not foremost regarding church attendance or even the long-term health of a congregation. The problem is that such parents neglect their duty as Christians and as Christian parents. Such neglect of duty only happens where

Christians are ignorant of their callings—along with their rights—to minister. Traditionally, the term for this concept has been *the priesthood of all believers*.

PIOUS MYTHS ASIDE

As the previous chapter argued, the public office of ministry is crucial. People must know whom to turn to for regular proclamation of the gospel, especially absolution. There is something important also about knowing that this person has some training and experience in pastoral work, has publicly committed (and thus is accountable) to it, and by virtue of a salary has time made available to do it. But the public office of ministry—in the presence or name of the assembly and related to a specific field of service—is not the whole of ministry.[1] It may not even be the better part of ministry. We overlook the full range of God's callings to ministry and the possibilities for ministry if we limit it to those who are in the ministerial office.

Let me say at the outset that this chapter is not about the ministry of "the laity" as such. It is about the ministry of *all Christians*. The priesthood of believers is not some part of the church set off from pastors. That is a "pious myth" originating in European Pietism. By virtue of faith and baptism, *all* Christians are priests; pastors don't forfeit their priesthood-of-believers card any more than they stop being believers at ordination (which I hope is a rare occurrence!). To pit pastors and the laity against each other, no matter which side one invests with power, is to damage the unity of the body of Christ that the priesthood of believers teaching is meant to recover.[2] A more productive way to think about the distinction in this chapter is the distinction between *vocations* and *callings* I discussed in chapter 3. A public minister of the church has a vocation, an office that commits her to consistent service in response to a ruling request: serve this congregation (or mission field) by public preaching of the word and administration of the sacraments. All baptized Christians, however, hear—and are anointed to respond to—callings of spiritual need from their neighbors, especially in "private" settings.

This way of approaching the issue should also make clear that when we are discussing the ministry of all believers, we are not talking about various worldly vocations or helpful activities as "ministry." According to a survey of Lutheran Church in America clergy and laity in 1982, about a third of the clergy and half of the laity regarded ministry chiefly as "everything done in life" or what "happens when people are helpful to others."[3] This is another pious myth that sometimes clouds the issue. I happen to be bivocational, so I have the benefit of seeing how this works from both angles. A few years ago, I was making small talk with a colleague at a conference for my academic administrative work. After telling her some of my history in seminary and church work, she asked, "Are you still involved in ministry?" But before she let me answer, she offered, "I suppose you think of your administrative work as ministry." This view arises from an insecurity among nonordained Christians that the daily tasks that fill their time are not righteous or at best are spiritually neutral. One sees it also in increasing propensity among nonordained Christians to speak of "feeling called" to particular fields of work—language that stems from the inner call notion historically associated with ordained ministry but ironically undercuts the distinctness of the ministerial office that the notion attempts to bolster (see chapter 4). But as Gerhard O. Forde wrote, "The fact that all are called to this ministry doesn't mean that everything the baptized do is to be called ministry. . . . It is best to avoid the current inflation in terminology which defines anything and everything Christians do as ministry."[4]

By applying what we have already discovered, especially in chapter 3, we recognize that we don't need to import some spiritual-sounding label to our worldly vocations to give them meaning. God is delighted that you teach children, work in HR, or build homes, even though it has nothing to do with your or anyone else's salvation.

A pious midwestern folktale tells of a young man who had a vision of the letters "P. C." in the night sky. He thought the divine message was to "Preach Christ." The letters, however, were actually telling him to "Plant Corn."[5] The supposed lesson is that planting corn is just as holy and divine a calling as preaching Christ. But in view of Luther's view of vocation and the priesthood of believers, that is a false dichotomy. The better interpretation is that the sign "P. C." in the sky means *both* "Plant Corn" *and* "Preach Christ." Commenting on "seek first the kingdom of God," Luther told his Wittenberg flock, "The kingdom of God requires you to do what you are commanded to do, to preach and to promote the Word of God, to serve your neighbor according to your calling, and to take whatever God gives you."[6] According to Luther, nonordained Christians had not only to deal with their "vocations" in the sense of worldly offices. They also bore the responsibilities to "preach and to promote the Word of God." In other words, they should expect to hear, and must respond to, calls to ministry.

WHAT DOES THIS MEAN?

People usually associate the priesthood of believers concept with Luther and the Protestant Reformation: Lutherans rejected the pope's and Roman priests' and bishops' unjust claims to power by asserting that all Christians (ordained and nonordained) are priests, with all the power and rights inherent in this priesthood. As most Lutherans appreciate, Luther was not inventing this argument for his own purposes but applying what he found in Scripture, particularly in 1 Peter 2:9:

> But you are a chosen race, a royal priesthood, a holy nation, God's own people, in order that you may proclaim the mighty acts of him who called you out of darkness into his marvelous light.

Few recognize, however, that Luther was not only recovering a biblical principle but reaffirming a basic Catholic teaching, albeit one that the church had downplayed or qualified into irrelevance.[7] Medieval church law preserved an anecdote, supposedly from Saint Augustine, in which two nonordained Christians—one who had committed a deadly sin and one who had not yet been baptized—found themselves on a sinking ship. The one with sin on his conscience baptized the other, who turned around and absolved his companion's sin.

Luther fleshed out the implications of this position early in the Reformation and maintained it consistently throughout his career. All Christians are born by baptism into the same single spiritual estate, or "walk of life." Luther rejected the Catholic notion that monks, nuns, priests, bishops, and popes constituted the "spiritual estate," while the nonordained were relegated to the "worldly estate."[8] For Luther, "spiritual" is just another way of saying that which comes about as a result of God's word. And since Christians are born of God's word, this word, and all its spiritual rights, powers, and duties, belongs equally to all Christians. For "when we grant the Word to anyone," said Luther, "we cannot deny anything to him pertaining to the exercise of his priesthood." Moreover, Christ, the true high priest, shares this priesthood with all his brothers and sisters, those who are united to him in baptism. Luther enumerated the "functions" of a priest as teaching and preaching, baptizing, administering the Lord's Supper, forgiving sins, praying for others, sacrificing, and judging doctrine and spirits.[9] In contrast to the Pietist and American evangelical construal of the priesthood of believers, the Lutheran doctrine is a "common priesthood," not an "individual priesthood" that emphasizes the believers' "soul competency" in religious matters or "direct access" to God without intermediaries.[10] In fact, nearly the opposite:

> If you want to be absolved from your sins in this manner, go to your pastor, or to your brother and neighbor if your pastor cannot hear you; he has the command to absolve you and comfort you. Do not invent a special absolution for yourself. . . . For God does not want us to go astray in our own self-chosen works or speculations.[11]

The doctrine of the universal priesthood affirms the right and duty of all Christians to function as intermediaries between God and their neighbors. The point is not some status Christians enjoy in an abstract sense but a set of functions we do for others; it is about action, not being.

PRIESTHOOD IN ACTION

We could undoubtedly gain much from elaborating on each of the functions of a priest as Luther saw it. I think it will be more beneficial to focus on teaching (and preaching), absolution, and judging doctrine. These functions tend to be the most neglected aspects of the universal priesthood that also have the potential for the greatest benefit in terms of bringing and sustaining others in faith.[12]

TEACHING AND PREACHING

In Acts 6, the Christian community in Jerusalem selected a man named Philip, along with six others, to help distribute food to widows. Many see this as the origin of the office of the deacon. While Christians have debated for decades the precise nature of this office and its relation to other offices, for our purposes, we note that Philip's vocation was to "serve tables" (KJV)—that is, extend charity and hospitality with the distribution of food. As Dorothea Wendebourg argues, "The diaconate has its own, specific task, quite independent of, and different from, that of the ordained ministry" in the sense of the "word and sacrament" of the Augsburg Confession.[13] Nevertheless, when Acts picks up Philip's story again two chapters later, he is preaching publicly in Samaria. He is also teaching the gospel in a one-on-one setting. Encountering an Ethiopian eunuch reading the prophet Isaiah, Philip asks the man if he understands what he is reading, and the Ethiopian replies, "How can I, unless someone guides me?" and invites Philip to read along with him. Philip then goes on to explain how the passage they are reading ("Like a sheep he was led to the slaughter") is about Jesus. The Ethiopian then goes one step further and asks to be baptized, which Philip dutifully does.

Whatever the nature of Philip's exact role in the early church, Acts gives no indication that he preached, taught, and baptized as part of his official vocation in the church.[14] He was, rather, exercising the functions of the universal priesthood in the context in which God placed him. In the case of his public preaching in Samaria, Philip, along with other Jerusalem Christians who had been "scattered" by persecution (Acts 8:4), found himself in a place without Christians. This is a textbook case of what Luther called "need[ing] no other call than to be a Christian, called and anointed by God from within." For here, necessity, duty, and love activate the right of all Christians to exercise the ministry of the word.[15] Furthermore, in the case of the Ethiopian, Philip was responding in love to a specific request—a calling of a neighbor in need of biblical teaching and baptism.

Luther's heirs have lost his clear perspective since the relationship between love and call was reframed during the age of orthodoxy, when Lutheran theologians felt obligated to argue the precise constitution of a "lawful call." For example, Johann Andreas Quenstedt, bound by his logical categories, stressed that a regular call is necessary for ministry.[16] He conceded that "in extreme necessity . . . every Christian is bound to teach, also without a call."[17] Yet to Quenstedt (unlike Luther), this was not a different kind of call (as Luther said, "called by God and anointed from within") but rather preaching *without* a call.

This distinction may be semantics. And it is possible that Quenstedt intended for the reader to infer that when he said Christians are obligated to teach in extreme necessity and do so "without a call," he meant without a *regular* call. But the difference in emphasis is telling. Whereas the orthodox theologian was concerned about the factors that *legitimized* ministry, Luther was concerned about the factors that *compelled* ministry. For Luther, whether in an emergency or not, love (understood as brotherly duty) moved the Christian to preach. Despite the well-meaning sentiment of the great Missouri Synod theologian Franz

Pieper that "all Christians . . . are spiritual priests and thus have the call to preach the Gospel," this may not be precise enough.[18] More accurate would be that all Christians are spiritual priests and thus have the right and duty to respond with the gospel when called upon—explicitly or implicitly as a function of one's office or as an unarticulated need among those who have never heard of Christ and have no access to the church's ministry. Both in the public office of ministry and as an exercise of the common priesthood, ministry is always offering God's word in response to a human call.

The lesson to learn from Philip's case begins with asking a simple question: Where has God placed me? The question is fundamentally vocational—which is to say, relational. *Where* God has placed you boils down to *whom* God has placed around you. As you look up from this book and survey your surroundings, you will see people, or the artifacts of people, whom God has placed in your midst. Probably 90 percent of these people will be family, friends, or coworkers. These are the people God has entrusted to us to hear and to respond to their requests for the teaching and preaching of God's word.

Perhaps many Christians are hesitant to teach and preach because they have a distorted idea of *what* exactly they should teach and preach. The pervasive influence of evangelical Christianity, with its stress on conversion or the "born-again" experience, seems to make "preaching" synonymous with speaking about one's own personal experience of God. When I was a Pentecostal Christian, I remember often, and with great gusto, singing a praise song called "Look What the Lord Has Done." A few of the lines go, "He healed my body / He touched my mind / He saved me just in time." Although the sentiment to testify to God's deliverance is thoroughly biblical (see, for example, Psalm 18), this kind of personal testimony too often takes the place of the proclamation of God's word. In Pentecostal circles at least, evangelism is often synonymous with "giving your testimony."

Practically speaking, the problem is twofold. First, if you don't feel like you have a personal story of God's dramatic deliverance—from a previous wicked life, from illness, from destitution—then you might feel like you have nothing to proclaim. This is compounded if your personal story is primarily of an emotional experience of God. I remember as a teenage Pentecostal feeling simultaneously eager to testify to my experience of Christ and slightly embarrassed because it meant I might have to defend a feeling, what at the time I considered an ineffable spiritual experience. Second, too much stress on personal experience makes the "testimony" vulnerable to human weakness. If my proclamation, for instance, is that God has turned my life around from alcoholism, what happens if I fall off the wagon? Either proclamation ceases or its credibility has been damaged, or both. At the end of the day, where such testimony is forced into the role of evangelism, it is "preaching ourselves," which the apostle Paul disavowed, precisely because of human weakness:

> For we do not proclaim ourselves; we proclaim Jesus Christ as Lord and ourselves as your slaves for Jesus' sake. For it is the God who said, "Let light shine out of darkness," who has shone in our hearts to give the light of the knowledge of the glory of God in the face of Jesus Christ. But we have this treasure in clay jars, so that it may be made clear that this extraordinary power belongs to God and does not come from us. (2 Cor 4:5–7)

The alternative to "preaching ourselves" is to "know nothing . . . except Jesus Christ, and him crucified" (1 Cor 2:2). This truth never changes, and it relies only on God's power. For this reason, Luther often described the task of preaching with the image (common in the paintings of his day) of John the Baptist with finger outstretched, pointing to Jesus and saying, "Here is the Lamb of God who takes away the sin of the world" (John 1:29).[19] With regard to preaching and teaching, the universal priesthood means that we Christians are to love our neighbors by offering this clear word to those whom God has placed in our lives. This brings us back to the story at the beginning of this chapter of the mother who intentionally refrained from requiring her children to attend church.

Parenthood is a fundamental vocation, upon which all other relationships of authority and obedience are built. As Luther wrote in the *Large Catechism*, "All other authority is derived and developed out of the authority of parents."[20] But it is not merely a "left-hand" or this-worldly vocation. Luther recognized "there is no greater or nobler authority on earth than that of parents over their children, for this authority is both spiritual and temporal." This meant, according to Luther, that "father and mother are apostles, bishops, and priests to their children . . . who make them acquainted with the gospel."[21] As Jane Strohl writes, parents are "the first and most pervasive witness to the Gospel their children experience."[22] Studies consistently show that parents' faith and religious support are significant factors in the faith of their children and that these effects carry into adulthood.[23] The only question is whether parents think their beliefs are something worth instilling in their children or whether we think our children's "freedom to choose" (which is a delusion) is more valuable than their salvation.[24]

As with all parenting tasks, the ministry of the word happens in structured and unstructured ways. Taking their cue from Deuteronomy 6:7 ("Recite [God's words] to your children"), Luther and his fellow Wittenberg leaders stressed the role of parents in teaching their children the basics of Christian faith.[25] Luther's *Small Catechism* explicitly directed the "head of the household" to teach the Commandments, the Apostles' Creed, the Lord's Prayer, baptism, the Lord's Supper, and daily prayers. The catechism was to be so woven into the home life that Luther's first publication of it was in poster form, or "broadsheets," meant to hang on the walls of the home and provide a focal point for instruction and conversation. Writers on vocation occasionally recognize this relationship to the priesthood of believers, especially in the context of families. Gene Edward Veith Jr. writes that "family devotions, Bible reading, moral instruction, and—especially important—the mutual forgiveness of sins and the proclamation and application of the Gospel are part of the spiritual formation of children that happens in the family."[26] Unfortunately, this connection between the priesthood of believers and vocations is rare or often misconstrued.

Luther had specific recommendations for how and how often this instruction occurred, but what matters most is that it is done at all. The task of teaching your children the faith may seem daunting, especially for those parents who worry that they don't have all the answers to faith questions that may arise. That may play into so many parents' decision to leave religious instruction to churches in Sunday school and confirmation or youth group. But as inadequate as the modern parent may feel, we should remember that Luther first proposed household instruction to parents he knew were illiterate or barely literate! What matters is that the process of instruction begins and begins early—that it becomes a routine and central feature of the home.

We all know how effortlessly young children learn words and actions. At the age of two years and seven months, my daughter learned to recite the Lord's Prayer after about a week of daily repetition. I incorporate not only prayers but teaching and proclamation into her bedtime routine, giving her the Aaronic blessing ("The Lord bless you and keep you"), the baptismal reminder ("Child of God, you are sealed with the Holy Spirit and marked with the cross of Christ forever"), and Paul's rapturous defiance of evil in Romans 8 ("If God is for you, who can be against you?"). The baptismal reminder comes with the sign of the cross on my daughter's forehead. And on more than one occasion, she has pulled herself out of the covers, stood up in her crib, and marked my forehead with the sign of the cross. Not only am I preaching to her, but she is proclaiming to me.

Influenced by twentieth-century educational theories, we sometimes worry about the effectiveness of "rote" memorization. Some might object that my young daughter hardly knew what she was doing when she marked me with Christ's cross or what she was saying as she mimicked the Lord's Prayer. But I would argue that this is an example of just what Luther has in mind when it comes to the priesthood of believers:

first, that the word of forgiveness comes to me from a brother or sister in Christ, and second, that children learn in their homes from an early age to offer forgiveness and pray habitually. Luther was so confident in the priesthood of believers that he advised people who were burdened in conscience to confess and receive absolution from a child if no preacher were available.[27] I, for one, want my daughter to have some practice for the time when that emergency comes. The real problems with memorization or habit only come when they are the end of education rather than the beginning. Through such practices as our bedtime prayer and proclamation routine and "Bible time," my daughter is spurred to ask questions and has begun to put things in her own words. Recently, her mother overheard our daughter—again, at just over two-and-a-half years old—opening a book about a big red dog but "reading" out loud a different story: "One day, God was big enough and then he was a little baby to be friends with the world." That, I dare say, is not a bad place to begin a lifelong conversation about the meaning of the incarnation.

The unstructured ministry of the word to our children is by nature less routine and takes more skill. In the flow of daily life, parents have opportunities to answer questions about God. They also learn to recognize when neighbors—in this case, our children—desire to hear God's word, even when they don't say it explicitly. Luther called this "the power of hearing the creature waiting"—that is, to recognize the often inarticulate "groans" of life as the creature's longing for God's redemption (Rom 8).[28] No precise program can be laid down for this. It may mean recognizing that a dangerous behavior calls for law or that a child's sulking—which is self-imposed punishment and what the medieval folk called *flagellation*—may be a call for forgiveness.

This unstructured ministry is also the bulk of ministry with other family members, friends, and coworkers. As Luther advised,

> Even though not everybody has the public office and calling, every Christian has the right and duty to teach, instruct, admonish,

comfort, and rebuke his neighbor with the Word of God at every opportunity and whenever necessary. For example, father and mother should do this for their children and household; a brother, neighbor, citizen or peasant for the other.[29]

Since mutual Christian love imposes obligations upon all, all Christians are obligated to preach and teach within their own vocations. This "mutual conversation and consolation," as Luther called it in the *Smalcald Articles*, is one of the ways, in addition to public preaching and the sacraments, that God is "extravagantly rich in his grace."[30] Through pastors, friends, and family who bear God's word when we are troubled, said Luther, "God runs after you."[31]

ABSOLUTION

Church tradition has often referred to absolution, or the pronouncement of God's forgiveness, as "binding and loosing sins" and "the power of the keys" (see Matt 16:19). Lutheran theology has always stressed that in the pronouncement of God's forgiveness, the sinner is *really* forgiven. Any condition or doubt throws the sinner back upon his own works or speculation. Furthermore, this forgiveness is not just some stale legal pronouncement; it is the opening of heaven. As much as in teaching, God runs after sinners through the universal priesthood in personal, often private, absolution.

Scholars have sometimes claimed that for all the freeing talk of vocation, Lutherans in the generations after the Reformation restricted women to their traditional roles as wives and mothers. But as Christopher B. Brown has shown, Lutheran leaders of the later sixteenth century defended the vocation of the midwife against Catholic attempts to restrict it. Moreover, their conception of this vocation is a great example of the priesthood of believers doctrine in action. Midwives naturally had the responsibilities of attending to the physical needs of mothers and children. But due to the sensibilities and medical realities of the time, they also took on direct spiritual roles, which the clergy encouraged. They were trained, and had access to manuals directing them, to baptize infants if their lives were in jeopardy and to pray for the mothers and offer words of comfort from Scripture. In more extreme cases where mothers' lives were at risk, midwives assumed "many of the functions otherwise associated exclusively with the clergy." Their ordinances for this situation called for a formula of absolution indistinguishable from the words pastors would proclaim in worship or in private confessions:

> And since you have made such a confession before me, and in true faith desire the grace of God and the forgiveness of your sins, I therefore, in the stead and by the command of Christ, hereby release and pronounce you free of all your sins, in the Name of God the Father, Son, and Holy Spirit. Amen.[32]

The early modern Lutheran midwife presents a helpful picture of how the priesthood of believers works in daily life. Our "worldly" vocations place us in situations where we hear the neighbor calling for more than our vocations technically offer. When that request—which may be implicit or explicit—is for God's word, Christians have the equal right and duty to offer that word, so long as it does not disrupt the good order of the church. These are as true and certain "calls to ministry" as any letter of call given by a congregation to a public minister.

Recently, my mother called me to update me on the details leading up to her decision to divorce her second husband, a man I never knew well because he had married my mom about a year after I left the house for college. When she finished her story, she paused before asking me bluntly, "So what do you think about my life right now?"

Masked in an uneasy chuckle, my mom's words were a clear indicator that she needed some straight talk. I'm not sure what she wanted to hear. More questions to show I was interested in her story? A vapid cliché, like "Things will work out"? What I feared she really wanted to hear was "It's not your fault; you're doing the right thing." While I was prepared to ask more questions, now was not the time. And no, I didn't know that things would work out. But most importantly, I was certain I could not tell her she was doing the right thing.

Instead, I heard the creature waiting. I had had similar conversations with my mom in the months prior, and in those conversations, I began to become bolder. I was not going to simply agree with everything she said. I was not going to let her put all the blame for her failing marriage on her husband. So I said things like "Well, you know, there's really no such thing as a 'no-fault divorce'; both people in a marriage are responsible for its health" and "When you are in couples therapy, how does he tell his side of the story?" And I had tried to nudge her in a gospel direction, telling her I hoped her pastor was not only offering good advice but also proclaiming forgiveness. But this time, I went further. She had literally asked me to make a judgment ("What do you think about my life right now?"). So I pronounced *God's* judgment: "This is not an easy situation," I said as calmly as I could. "And I know it's not where you want your life to be right now, but remember, Mom, that you are forgiven through Jesus Christ."

I should state forthrightly that in such an offer of absolution, I was acting in my capacity not as an ordained minister but as a brother in Christ. My official call commits me to a specific congregation. Although my ministerial training undoubtedly equipped and emboldened me to speak forgiveness in this situation, the whole point is that all brothers and sisters in Christ should learn to hear the creature waiting.

And I pray that I am also heard in my waiting. The Lutheran tradition of confession and absolution in every worship service is a life-saving practice. But sometimes the burden on one's conscience calls for immediate forgiveness. Not long ago, I came home from work with a heavy heart. I had had a major miscommunication with my supervisor, who I felt was reading my behavior uncharitably. On the surface, my concern was to repair communication with my supervisor for the sake of our relationship, our shared work, and—of course—my continued employment. But more deeply, I sensed a resentment rising within me, a classic case of being "angry with a brother or sister" that Jesus classifies as murder (Matt 5:21–22). After venting, as spouses often do in these situations, I recognized what I really needed. "Will you give me forgiveness?" I asked my wife. She did, and I was forgiven. What occurred between us was exactly what Luther spoke of:

> We all have the power, but no one should presume to exercise it publicly except for him who is chosen by the congregation. Privately however, I may indeed make use of it. For example, when my neighbor comes, saying "Dear friend, my conscience is burdened; speak an Absolution to me," I may do so freely, but it must happen privately.[33]

In short, my wife heard and responded to the call to ministry.

All Christians need absolution. Perhaps ministers feel this need more acutely, since they are more often the ones proclaiming absolution for others. The need for absolution is not lessened by being a skilled theologian or practitioner of "devotional" practices. Luther himself recognized his need for simple scriptural comfort:

> I am indeed a Doctor of Theology and many tell me that they were signally advanced in their knowledge of Holy Scripture through my help. But I have also experienced that I was helped and cheered through a single word of a brother who believed himself to be in no sense my equal. There is tremendous weight in the word of a brother which, in an hour of emergency, he adduces from Scripture.[34]

The longing of pastors for absolution and encouragement hit home for me in a recent area pastors' meeting. One of my colleagues was describing a difficult scenario he recently encountered in which a parishioner had a major health incident before the worship service. After duly attending to the emergency, the pastor hurried to start the service. He admitted that he felt he "didn't do right" by rushing to the service—presumably rather than lingering to offer more informal pastoral support to those who witnessed and were involved in the incident. Regardless of whether he made a wise choice in that moment, his conscience was clearly burdened. As we were meeting over Zoom, I typed a direct message to this pastor, asking if he would like absolution, for "after all, we're all pastors"—by which I meant that we were all experienced and trained to offer absolution. He did not reply, either because he didn't see the chat message (they can be easy to miss) or because he did not want absolution in that moment.

The universal priesthood's functions of teaching, preaching, and absolution take on a crucial role considering realities facing the church in the United States today. Proclamation must be central to the church's collective response to the pronounced decline in church membership—a claim, of course, that does not deny the infinite value of proclaiming God's word to any single individual. According to Gallup polls, between the polling cycles of 1998–2000 and 2016–18, all generations showed a roughly 10 percent drop in church membership. And the youngest adults are by far the least religious, meaning that even if emerging generations join churches at the same rate as millennials, overall membership will continue to decline as the older generations die.[35] The Evangelical Lutheran Church in America (ELCA), for instance, has steadily lost members since its founding in 1987. Beginning with about 5.2 million members, the ELCA now claims just over 3 million. The downward trend is expected only to accelerate in the coming decades, so the ELCA "will basically cease to exist within the next generation."[36]

Of course, it's debatable whether such doomsday rhetoric is productive. And we should be cautious not to equate "the church" with any organization or set of organizations. But the facts are clear: church membership is shrinking. And insofar as church membership has some correlation to the number of believers (the true, hidden "church"), we should be concerned. Since faith comes by hearing (Rom 10:17), "the church is a creature of the gospel," as Luther said.[37] Faith is always up to the Holy Spirit, but we know that the Holy Spirit uses the proclamation of God's word. Reverse engineered, a core response to the decline of the church is just as clear: the church should be proclaiming more, for "where the word is, there is the church."[38] That is to say, where we wish the church to be, we speak it.

More ordained ministers should be part of this effort, but so should a newly emboldened and trained priesthood of all believers. The need for "mutual conversation and consolation"—brothers and sisters in Christ teaching, preaching, and absolving one another—will only grow, especially as fewer people enter ordained ministry and fewer churches can afford a full-time pastor. A part-time pastor, for instance, often means a bivocational pastor, which is not itself a bad thing. But it comes with certain limitations. When your pastor is working a second job, she may not be able to come as quickly in a pastoral emergency.[39] In those situations, the church needs believers who are accustomed to comforting one another with God's word—always complementary to and never in competition with the public office of ministry.

JUDGING

Another way the universal priesthood works in cooperation with the public office of ministry is in making sure that the office is filled—and filled with those who proclaim God's pure word. Partly this is a matter of each one having "regard for his own salvation," since each person stands individually accountable before God, and listening to a false teacher is no excuse. But Luther's utmost concern was that the *community* should see to it that "souls would not perish for lack of the divine word."[40] In Christian love, we have a duty to one another to ensure that God's word is proclaimed in our midst. This requires that the community take responsibility for judging teachers, both before they are called to ministerial office and while they are in office.

The right and duty of all believers to judge teaching is founded on the doctrine of the common priesthood. But Luther's scriptural argument tended to be more direct. God's word commands Christians to "test everything; hold fast to what is good" (1 Thess 5:21) and "beware of false prophets" (Matt 7:15). Luther's logic was simple: "How could one beware of false prophets if one did not consider and judge their teaching?"[41]

In practice, the duty to judge teaching and provide ministers may not fall equally to all. Human customs and institutional structures may mean some members of the community have more authority and opportunity than others to ensure that the office of public ministry is responsibly filled. In fact, Luther first worked out his notions of the common priesthood in an effort to rouse Christian secular rulers to protect their subjects from Rome's abuse and exploitation, including being deprived of competent preachers. Luther objected to the way the Catholic leadership arrogated to itself the sole authority to judge doctrine. And although having hierarchical structures for electing church leaders is not wrong in itself, it is problematic if the hierarchy claims the sole ability to do this while impeding the gospel. So as "fellow-Christians, fellow-priests, fellow-members of the spiritual estate, fellow-lords over all things," Christian civil authorities have the same duty as all believers to judge teaching and in fact may be well positioned to counteract error.[42]

Modern American Christians may see such involvement in church affairs by secular authorities as an intrusion, but for Luther, it was a matter of Christian love and service that rulers have "true spiritual courage to do the best they can for the poor church."[43] In societies where church and state are more clearly separated, other Christians will emerge as the leaders with these responsibilities. Congregations elect church councils and appoint call committees, which are made publicly accountable for ensuring public ministry. They cooperate with larger denominational structures, such as candidacy committees and synod and district staff, to determine the best qualified candidates for pastoral office. In the healthiest scenarios, the congregation as a whole gets a voice and perhaps also a vote. At every level of this decision-making, the church is exercising the rights and duties of the common priest-hood. For this work to be a meaningful assurance of public ministry in the gospel sense (and not a rubber stamp or a decision based on extrinsic qualities like personality or appearance), all those involved must be aware that the work is fundamentally passing judgment on teaching. The minister's (or potential minister's) doctrine is on display through conversations, writing, teaching sessions, and sermons. As should be clear from previous chapters, this judging work does not include interrogating the subject's sense of an inner call.

American Christians today may not live with the same threat Luther encountered of being denied pure gospel preachers. So they may wonder if it is really necessary for *all* Christians to be invested in judging teaching. Can't we trust our pastors and denominational officials to do this for us? But aside from the general biblical commandment to "test the spirits" (1 John 4:1), two considerations urge this work upon all believers.

First, specific circumstances can put congregations in the position of needing to make ministry decisions frequently and with limited support from denominational officials. Smaller congregations in particular, because they may not be able to afford full-time ministers, may have persistent pastoral turnover or long gaps between called pastors. This creates significant work for congregational leaders, in which case it may be wise to frequently rotate those serving on such committees. The congregation I currently serve (as a part-time pastor) has a history of needing to scramble to provide public ministry. Unable to afford a full-time pastor and located in a rural area without a surplus of Lutheran ministers, the congregation was for years served by retired pastors (who did not commit to preaching every week), occasional "lay ministers," and extended "pulpit supply" from seminarians. The congregation was seemingly in the active work of ensuring public ministry for decades. The chair of the ministry committee, who was in her late seventies when I began to serve, took it almost as her personal task to provide for public ministry, making calls weekly and even providing visiting ministers a place to sleep. Given the church membership decline noted above, smaller churches facing these issues are only going to increase. But it's not only small churches that may find themselves in such situations. As any congregation that has been through rapid pastoral turnover due to scandal or other drama knows, sometimes congregations are actively involved for years in the work of filling the ministerial office. The more the church as a whole understands its obligations as the common spiritual priesthood, the more this burden can be shared and the work fulfilled responsibly. And the more Christians see their lives vocationally, as laid out in chapter 3, the more readily and joyfully will they respond to calls from their neighbors to serve in these roles within their congregations.

Second, approval and a call to ministry do not ensure a pastor's ongoing faithfulness to the gospel. As Luther and the orthodox writers often stated, the regular call is a great comfort for congregants, for such a minister, being authorized by Christ's body, speaks with the authority of Christ. But as crucial as a regular call is for the public office of ministry, it does not guarantee a valid ministry. The "order" inherent in a regular call was worthless, said Luther, if the gospel were not proclaimed, for "the office . . . . extends no farther than the Word goes."[44] Christ's warning against "thieves and bandits" in John 10 "refer[s] in general to all those—even to them who have a true call and are regularly installed in office—who do not begin with and adhere to the doctrine of faith in Christ."[45] This is why hearers are entrusted with judging teachings, for the sheep know the voice of the true shepherd. For the sake of their own and their neighbors' salvation, all Christians must vigilantly judge the preaching they hear and be ready to take necessary action to protect themselves and others from error. "Wherever there is a Christian congregation in possession of the gospel," wrote Luther,

it not only has the right and power but also the duty—on pain of losing the salvation of its souls and in accordance with the promise made to Christ in baptism—to avoid, to flee, to depose, and to withdraw from the authority [of those who] . . . teach and rule contrary to God and his word.[46]

When faced with ministers who impede God's word or substitute human teachings for divine proclamation, Christians are duty bound to remove themselves or the offending minister. In the same way that a civil administrator—similarly entrusted with what is common to all—is removable if he is unfaithful, a pastor is "more readily removable," since a civil officer deals with temporal matters, while a gospel minister handles "eternal possessions."[47]

Luther was confident that the sheep have "very keen ears" and can distinguish the voice of the true shepherd from thieves and bandits.[48] In fact, "a Christian is so certain about what he ought and ought not believe that he will even die, or at least be prepared to die, for it."[49] Such certainty may sound naive, especially given the apparent lack of basic theological and biblical knowledge among churchgoers. A classic study from a generation ago found that a third of Lutherans lacked a "rudimentary understanding of the gospel," 40 percent adhered to salvation by works, and 70 percent said that all religions lead to the same God.[50] More recent Pew Research Center data found that less than half of US Protestants agree that salvation is by "faith alone," with closer to a third of mainline Protestants agreeing with this core Lutheran teaching.[51]

With such underwhelming statistics on theological understanding and conviction among churchgoers, entrusting the church as a whole with judging its preachers and teachers may seem foolhardy. But Luther would remind us that it is not *we* who are entrusting this task to the church at large but *Christ*. Luther's controversy with the Catholic Church of his day revealed that the church itself—that is, the priesthood of believers—is always the only defense against false teaching. This is not because the church is somehow more inherently apt than leadership (this would be a false dichotomy between church and leadership) but because the church is the gospel's creature. Although human custom may delegate certain duties to the clergy, it never forfeits its

right to ensure gospel ministry, as Philip Melanchthon stated classi-
cally in his *Treatise on the Power and Primacy of the Pope*.[52] We should,
therefore, be more willing to trust that the Holy Spirit equips God's
sheep with "keen ears."

But this doesn't mean the church and its leaders should blithely
assume the church will exercise its priesthood in judging teaching.
First, preachers need to preach the gospel. Where they fail at this, the
Good Shepherd will have no sheep. Without the gospel melody already
filling their ears, they will not be able to recognize preaching that
matches its pitch. Second, the church needs to teach believers about
the rights and duties inherent in the common priesthood. Although
authority is to be respected, believers need to know their own authority, that they in fact have power, like the apostle Paul, to curse angels
if they should bring a foreign gospel and correct bishops if they con-
tradict God's word.[53] Whether this is public ministers teaching their
congregations or members teaching one another is immaterial. How
many church members sit under preaching that is only law, self-help, or
feel-goodism without making their concerns known?

Certainly, any challenge to the public minister should be handled
with love and avoidance of scandal, following Matthew 18:15–20. But
at the end of the day, such judgment cannot be shirked. For one thing, as
Luther wrote, "the need of souls compels it."[54] We owe our brothers
and sisters in Christ—especially those weak in faith—a reliable supply
of gospel proclamation. Furthermore, as with all things that matter to
God, the law threatens us if we disobey Christ's clear command. The
hearers, according to Luther, "not only have the power and the right to
judge everything that is preached, they also have the duty to judge, on
pain of [incurring] the disfavor of Divine Majesty."[55] Where Christians
are not moved by love, God moves with warnings.

The positive side of this work of judging teaching is the responsibility to care for those in the public office of ministry. Ministers need
support, encouragement, and resources to do their work well, to fulfill
their God-given vocations. The work of ensuring ministry does not end

with hiring a pastor. Rather than the appeal to the universal priesthood that is sometimes antagonistic to ordained ministry, this doctrine really aims at reinforcing the unity and complementarity of the body of Christ. Just as pastors should equip parishioners in faithful service in their vocations, so parishioners have a responsibility to equip their pastors for their vocations. This would also extend to the auxiliary functions and resources that support this ministry. As Timothy J. Wengert writes, "If someone wants to invoke Luther's understanding of the universal, spiritual priesthood properly, it should be to urge paying a higher percentage of one's salary to support the pastor or fix the leaks in the parsonage roof."[56]

The goal is not, of course, the comfort of the minister but ensuring that the ministerial office is competently filled for the sake of salvation and edification for all. In honest conversation, the pastor and the congregation determine what this support looks like. A church does well to consider the minister's salary and benefits, ongoing education, and extended time for study or retreat. Remembering that the essential work of the ministerial office is proclaiming God's word and administering the sacraments, the congregation should also carefully consider its expectations of its minister. To the extent that the congregation members can assume administrative, social, and programmatic responsibilities, they free their minister to focus on the core work of preaching and offering the sacraments. This is precisely what the early church in Jerusalem did by appointing servants to distribute food to the needy (Acts 6:1–6).[57] My own congregation succeeds in this, with hospitality groups, an altar guild, and other services operating largely without my involvement. Again, this is particularly helpful for a part-time minister, since it allows me to focus my limited time on preaching, teaching, sacramental ministry, and pastoral care. On the other hand, if ministers take advantage of this freedom to neglect their duties, they fall under judgment.

As Lutherans have long taught, God gives the ministry of his word to the whole church. Since all Christians—public ministers or not—are priests, no Christian lacks the ministry of the word. And God demands Christians serve others with the word; they can no more neglect to provide God's word to others than they can neglect the physical needs of a destitute neighbor. In fact, the duty to provide God's word is greater because it deals with eternity. Those who are not in the office of public ministry are often directly involved in this ministry, especially in teaching their families and absolving one another's sins when called upon and a pastor is not at hand. But these believers also have a crucial indirect role in ministry through judging teaching—that is, supporting and holding accountable public ministers. A recovery of this obligation and boldness to minister and support ministry not only is faithful to Scripture, the logic of the gospel, and Lutheran tradition but also holds much promise for a church that faces a declining membership and a dwindling supply of pastors.

* * *

Gospel ministry—in all its forms, both public and private, performed by ordained or nonordained Christians—is only rightly understood if it is understood *vocationally*. As this book has argued, this means God calling directly to you through neighbors in need. God gets you to serve needy people around you through particular in-the-moment requests (what I have called "callings") and publicly recognized offices and relationships (what I have called "vocations"). To ask whether one has a passion for the work, feels called to it, or is fulfilled in it is to overlook the fact that God commands it and promises to sustain those who do it: "He will command his angels concerning you to guard you in all your ways" (Ps 91:11). The long history of the "inner call" theory in Lutheranism is unfortunate because it threatens the *common* priesthood of believers, especially as it suggests the call to be some kind of permanent possession or condition of the individual or is taken to mean the individual knows the ministry to be the vocation in which he can be most useful. Just as troubling, the inner call theory untethers the theology of ministerial call from the doctrine of vocation. But the church has inherited a treasure in Luther's clear vision of how God normally gets his word proclaimed. This ministry is set in motion as any other calling or vocation, simply by hearing and responding to real, physical human requests—not abstractions of need or perceived internal communication from God. As fellow priests, all believers have an equal right and duty to respond to these requests, even while some are designated to do it publicly, reliably, and in an ongoing way in response to implicit requests, such as preaching every Sunday. If this way of thinking about ministry seems a bit too mundane, unromantic, or unspiritual, it may be that we are not appreciating what ministry accomplishes. Ministry is the only vocation of the old world of sin that exists to bring people into the new world of righteousness. Herein lies its spirituality.

When I was progressing through the process of becoming ordained, I was caught off guard by the request to articulate my inner call to ministry. Some may feel the same, and others who have objections or reservations about the notion may be tempted to perjure themselves to move on in the process. I offer this book as historical and theological support for those who are uncomfortable with the concept. Of course, others may go along without giving the issue much thought, and many probably are convinced they sense an inner call. To these—as well as to the denominational leaders and church structures that perpetuate the inner call requirement—I offer this book as a challenge. The church has no basis in Scripture, Luther, or the Lutheran confessions to expect an inner call of ministers or consider it valid (even if not sufficient) without supernatural confirmation. The time has come to set aside such a notion and return our theology of ministerial call to its proper place: squarely in the context of vocation and the priesthood of all believers.

Acknowledgments

The irony of writing a book about vocation—especially if none of your vocations entails writing books about such a thing—is that it takes time and attention away from other vocations. My first note of gratitude, therefore, goes to my wife, Gina, and daughter, Margot, for enduring my absences while I worked on this project. I extend a similar word of thanks to the community of faith at St. John Lutheran Church. Although working on this book did not technically pull me away from pastoral duties, my absorption in this project likely caused my work to suffer in subtle ways.

I can thank my wife and several members of St. John for more than their sacrifices of my time and attention. Gina helpfully read the entire manuscript, giving valuable suggestions from the nonspecialist perspective. The adult Sunday school read and discussed an earlier draft of this book, helping me appreciate how nonordained members of the priesthood of believers might wrestle with the ideas presented here.

Several scholars generously answered the call to read parts or the whole of earlier drafts: David Whitford, Mark Granquist, and Andrew Ronnevik. For their expertise and encouragement, I am grateful. For any lingering errors or inadequacies in this book, I remain responsible.

Finally, librarians and archivists have provided me with crucial materials. I am grateful to the interlibrary loan staff at Baylor University, Joel Thoreson at the archives of the Evangelical Lutheran Church in America, and Brigid Miller at St. Olaf College archives.

Notes

Introduction

1 Robert Kolb and Timothy J. Wengert, eds., *The Book of Concord: The Confessions of the Evangelical Lutheran Church* (Minneapolis: Fortress, 2000), 46 (hereafter cited as *BC*).

2 David J. Peter, "A Lutheran Perspective on the Inward Call to the Ministry," *Concordia Journal* 12, no. 4 (July 1986): 125.

3 For as large as the inner call concept looms in some Lutheran circles today, very little scholarly work exists on it. In the context of a discussion of article 14 of the Augsburg Confession, Timothy J. Wengert briefly (in a footnote) critiques the way some in the ELCA "completely overemphasize the 'internal call.'" Timothy J. Wengert, *The Augsburg Confession: Renewing Lutheran Faith and Practice* (Minneapolis: Fortress, 2020), 128n4. More typically, histories of the doctrine of the ministry in Lutheranism fail to deal with the concept. For example, James H. Pragman, *Traditions of Ministry: A History of the Doctrine of the Ministry in Lutheran Theology* (St. Louis: Concordia, 1983); John C. Wohlrabe, "An Historical Analysis of the Doctrine of the Ministry in the Lutheran Church–Missouri Synod until 1962" (ThD diss., Concordia Seminary, 1987); and Eugene F. A. Klug, *Church and Ministry: The Role of Church, Pastor, and People from Luther to Walther* (St. Louis: Concordia, 1993). See also the historical essays in Todd W. Nichol and Marc Kolden, eds., *Called*

and Ordained: Lutheran Perspectives on the Office of the Ministry (Minneapolis: Fortress, 1990). Lutheran theologians and Bible scholars almost always ignore the issue, dealing as they are with issues considered more pressing, like episcopacy and women's ordination. For example, Roy A. Harrisville, Ministry in Crisis: Changing Perspectives on Ordination and the Priesthood of All Believers (Minneapolis: Augsburg, 1987); and John Henry Paul Reumann, Ministries Examined: Laity, Clergy, Women, and Bishops in a Time of Change (Minneapolis: Augsburg, 1987).

4 "The Call Process Handbook," Evangelical Lutheran Church in America (ELCA), Northern Texas–Northern Louisiana Mission Area, 2012, 5, https://www.ntnl.org/wp-content/uploads/2015/05/CPHandbookv8.pdf.

5 For instance, Todd W. Nichol claims that American Lutherans have generally agreed that "the call to the public ministry normally originates in the Christian congregation." Todd W. Nichol, "Ministry and Oversight in American Lutheranism," in Nichol and Kolden, Called and Ordained, 94. Also, Evangelical Lutheran Synod leader John A. Molstad Jr. wrote in 2003 that Lutherans have used the expression "inner call" "very sparingly." John A. Molstad Jr., "The Pastor's Proper Handling of Call," Bethany Lutheran Theological Seminary, 2003, http://www.blts.edu/wp-content/uploads/2011/06/JAM-Call.pdf.

Chapter 1: European Foundations

1 Carter Lindberg, "Conflicting Models of Ministry: Luther, Karlstadt, and Muentzer," Concordia Theological Quarterly 41, no. 4 (October 1977): 36.

2 BC, 467.

3 Martin Luther, Luther's Works, ed. Jaroslav Pelikan and Helmut T. Lehmann, American ed., 55 vols. (Philadelphia: Fortress; St. Louis: Concordia, 1955–86), 40:176 (hereafter cited as LW).

4 For "tortured," see LW 37:41. Zwingli admitted he had to "press and squeeze" Christ's words to be rendered as "This is the sign of my body." LW 37:145 (emphasis added). For "offended," see LW 37:70–71.

5 LW 37:94.

6 LW 37:136.

7 LW 37:219.

8 LW 37:95.

9 Ewald M. Plass, ed., *What Luther Says: An Anthology* (St. Louis: Concordia, 1959), 3:1125, citing Martin Luther, *Luthers Werke: Kritische Gesamtausgabe* [Schriften], 73 vols. (Weimar, Germany: H. Böhlau, 1883–2009), 47:229 (hereafter cited as WA).

10 LW 2:272.

11 LW 53:125.

12 LW 40:385.

13 LW 25:447.

14 Wilhelm Maurer, *Historical Commentary on the Augsburg Confession*, trans. H. George Anderson (Philadelphia: Fortress, 1986), 193.

15 LW 39:312. On Luther's recommendation for ordination for presiding at the Eucharist, see Arthur Carl Piepkorn, "The Sacred Ministry and Holy Ordination in the Symbolical Books of the Lutheran Church," *Concordia Theological Monthly* 40, no. 8 (1969): 555.

16 LW 40:21.

17 LW 40:34. See also LW 13:332; and John Nicholas Lenker, ed., *Sermons of Martin Luther: The Church Postils*, vols. 3–4 (Grand Rapids, MI: Baker, 1995), 3:374.

18 LW 13:329.

19 LW 13:66.

20 Ewald M. Plass, ed., *What Luther Says: An Anthology* (St. Louis: Concordia, 1959), 2:947, citing WA 40.1:59–60.

21 LW 40:384.

22 LW 40:113. See also LW 40:195, 222, 384. Properly speaking, this was, in Luther's mind, a sending rather than a calling, although Luther did not press the distinction. See Lenker, *Sermons of Martin Luther*, 4:254. See also Lenker, 4:271.

23 Lenker, 4:252. See also Lenker, 4:270.

24 Lenker, 4:271.

25 Lenker, 4:252–53.

26 LW 39:310. See also LW 40:36.

27 LW 40:38. See also LW 39:312.

28 LW 40:36.

29 Lenker, *Sermons of Martin Luther*, 4:254.

30 LW 40:52.

31 In fact, the previous Orlamünde pastor had resigned, and the Orlamünde parish had requested Karlstadt as its pastor. The terms upon which Karlstadt took this work were complicated by many factors, presenting abundant opportunities for misunderstanding. For instance, that Karlstadt was so enthusiastically supported by the people of Orlamünde before he took the pulpit there makes it possible that Karlstadt, who traveled much during this time, had sown seeds of dissension toward the incumbent. Also, the Orlamünde parish had been a sinecure of Karlstadt, meaning Karlstadt was legally owed income from the parish, but due to mismanagement, Karlstadt had not received much of it. And when Elector Frederick granted Orlamünde to Karlstadt, he was not clear if this meant Karlstadt was to resign his archdeaconate, in terms of both its income and its lecturing duties at Wittenberg; Karlstadt eventually claimed the income but did not continue lecturing. Furthermore, the University at Wittenberg inexplicably was not consulted on the pastoral change. Ronald J. Sider, *Andreas Bodenstein von Karlstadt: The Development of His Thought, 1517–1525*, Studies in Medieval Thought 11 (Leiden: Brill, 1974), 180–88.

32 LW 40:116.

33 LW 40:135.

34 Cited in Sider, *Andreas Bodenstein von Karlstadt*, 295–96.

35 Amy Nelson Burnett, ed., *The Eucharistic Pamphlets of Andreas Bodenstein von Karlstadt* (Kirksville, MO: Truman State University Press, 2011), 133.

36 Burnett, 210. See also Amy Nelson Burnett, *Karlstadt and the Origins of the Eucharistic Controversy: A Study in the Circulation of Ideas* (New York: Oxford University Press, 2011), 62.

37 Cited in Sider, *Andreas Bodenstein von Karlstadt*, 233.

38 Sider, 267.

39 Edward J. Furcha, ed., *The Essential Carlstadt: Fifteen Tracts*, Classics of the Radical Reformation 8 (Scottdale, PA: Herald, 1995), 178.

40 Furcha, 172.

41 Furcha, 175, 179.

42 Furcha, 177, 178.

43 Furcha, 177, 178, 175.

44 BC, 340–41.

45 BC, 341.

46 BC, 220–21. See also Piepkorn, "Sacred Ministry," 554.

47 John Calvin, *Institutes of the Christian Religion*, ed. John T. McNeill, trans. Ford Lewis Battles, Library of Christian Classics (Philadelphia: Westminster, 1960), 21:1382 (IV.17.19).

48 Calvin, 21:1391 (IV.17.24).

49 This was the view of Heinrich Bullinger. See Bruce Gordon, *Calvin* (New Haven, CT: Yale University Press, 2009), 240.

50 Calvin, *Institutes*, 21:1372 (IV.17.11); Calvin, 21:1400 (IV.17.29); Calvin, 21:1385 (IV.17.20); Calvin, 21:1381 (IV.17.18); Calvin, 21:1403 (IV.17.31).

51 J. Mark Beach, "The Real Presence of Christ in the Preaching of the Gospel: Luther and Calvin on the Nature of Preaching," *Mid-America Journal of Theology* 10 (1999): 97–100. The quote is from p. 99.

52 Calvin, *Institutes*, 21:1054 (IV.3.1).

53 Calvin, 21:1062–63 (IV.3.10).

54 John Calvin, *Commentaries on the Book of the Prophet Jeremiah and the Lamentations*, ed. John Owen (Grand Rapids, MI: Christian Classics Ethereal Library, n.d.), 3:Jer 23:21, https://www.ccel.org/ccel/calvin/calcom19.pdf.

55 Calvin, *Institutes*, 21:1062 (IV.3.2).

56 J. F. Puglisi, *The Process of Admission to Ordained Ministry: A Comparative Study*, trans. Michael S. Driscoll and Mary Misrahi (Collegeville, MN: Liturgical, 1996), 2:107.

57 Calvin, *Institutes*, 21:1063 (IV.3.11).

58 Calvin, *Commentaries*, 3:Jer 23:21.

59 Johann Gerhard, *On the Ministry I—Theological Commonplaces*, ed. Benjamin T. G. Mayes, trans. Richard J. Dinda (St. Louis: Concordia, 2012), 86. See also Johann Andreas Quenstedt, *The Holy Ministry*, trans. Luther Poellot (Fort Wayne, IN: Concordia Theological Seminary Press, 1991), 8.

60 Quenstedt, *Holy Ministry*, 3, 25, 29.

61 Quenstedt, 7.

62 The distinction was not always so tidy. See Gerhard, *On the Ministry*, 151; Heinrich Schmid, *The Doctrinal Theology of the Evangelical*

Lutheran Church: Exhibited, and Verified from the Original Sources, trans. Charles A. Hay and Henry Eyster Jacobs (Philadelphia: Lutheran Publication Society, 1876), 624; and Timothy Schmeling, ed., *Lives and Writings of the Great Fathers of the Lutheran Church* (St. Louis: Concordia, 2016), 143.

63 Quenstedt, *Holy Ministry*, 9.

64 Gerhard, *On the Ministry*, 106.

65 Leonard Hutter, *Compend of Lutheran Theology: A Summary of Christian Doctrine, Derived from the Word of God and the Symbolical Books of the Evangelical Lutheran Church,* trans. Henry Eyster Jacobs and George Frederick Spieker (Philadelphia: Lutheran Book Store, 1868), 143.

66 Martin Chemnitz, *Loci Theologici,* trans. Jacob A. O. Preus (St. Louis: Concordia, 1989), 699. See also Martin Chemnitz, *Ministry, Word, and Sacraments: An Enchiridion,* trans. Luther Poellot (St. Louis: Concordia, 1981), 30–31.

67 For instance, Gerhard, *On the Ministry,* 116–18.

68 Chemnitz, *Loci Theologici,* 701.

69 Chemnitz, *Ministry, Word, and Sacraments,* 29.

70 Chemnitz, 31, 32; Quenstedt, *Holy Ministry,* 3–4.

71 Chemnitz, *Loci Theologici,* 700.

72 Gerhard, *On the Ministry,* 109.

73 Johann Andreas Quenstedt, *The Nature and Character of Theology: An Introduction to the Thought of J. A. Quenstedt from Theologia Didactico-Polemica Sive Systema Theologicum* (St. Louis: Concordia, 1986), 193. See also Quenstedt, *Holy Ministry,* 8.

74 Chemnitz, *Ministry, Word, and Sacraments,* 28.

75 Gerhard, *On the Ministry,* 238.

76 Gerhard, 101.

77 Chemnitz, *Ministry, Word, and Sacraments,* 123–26, 133; Quenstedt, *Holy Ministry,* 35, 37.

78 Joar Haga, *Was There a Lutheran Metaphysics? The Interpretation of Communicatio Idiomatum in Early Modern Lutheranism* (Göttingen, Germany: Vandenhoeck & Ruprecht, 2012), 130–212. The quote is from p. 170. See BC, 631; Werner Elert, *The Structure of Lutheranism* (St. Louis: Concordia, 2003), 222–36; and Schmid, *Doctrinal Theology,* 355–57.

79 "Eclectic Lutheran spirituality" is from R. Daniel Van Voorhis, "A Prophet of Interior Lutheranism: The Correspondence of Johann Arndt" (PhD diss., University of St. Andrews, 2008), 133.

80 Peter C. Erb, trans. and ed., *Johann Arndt: True Christianity* (New York: Paulist, 1979), 14, cited in Eric Lund, *Documents from the History of Lutheranism, 1517–1750* (Minneapolis: Augsburg Fortress, 2002), 256.

81 Van Voorhis, "Prophet of Interior Lutheranism," 99.

82 Cited in Robert A. Kelly, "True Repentance and Sorrow: Johann Arndt's Doctrine of Justification," *Consensus* 16, no. 2 (1990): 58.

83 Lund, *History of Lutheranism*, 257.

84 Van Voorhis, "Prophet of Interior Lutheranism," 168.

85 Cited in Kent Brauer Burreson, "Ordination Liturgies, the Call Process, and the Office of the Ministry in the Landeskirche of Braunschweig-Wolfenbuttel, 1569–1815" (STM thesis, Concordia Seminary, 1994), 124.

86 The church order of Mecklenburg, 1552, cited in Elert, *Structure of Lutheranism*, 353.

87 W. van 't Spijker, *The Ecclesiastical Offices in the Thought of Martin Bucer* (Leiden: Brill, 1996), 393; Puglisi, *Admission to Ordained Ministry*, 2:98, 106, 117.

88 Jonathan Strom, *Orthodoxy and Reform: The Clergy in Seventeenth Century Rostock* (Tubingen: Mohr Siebeck, 1999), 91–92.

89 Paul Tarnow, *De Sacrosancto Ministerio, Libri Tres* (Rostock, Germany, 1624), 63, 65, 66, 67.

90 Johann Friedrich Mayer, *Museum Ministri Ecclesiae* (Leipzig, 1690), 7, 28, 10, 33, 39, 63.

91 Johann Fecht, *Instructio Pastoralis* (Rostock, Germany, 1728), 11, 23.

92 Philipp Jakob Spener, "The Spiritual Priesthood," in *Hauptschriften*, ed. Paul Grünberg (Gotha, Germany, 1889), question 26, cited in Peter C. Erb, ed., *Pietists: Selected Writings* (New York: Paulist, 1983), 54.

93 Philipp Jakob Spener, *Pia Desideria*, trans. Theodore G. Tappert (Philadelphia: Fortress, 1964), 93.

94 Philipp Jakob Spener, *Theologische Bedencken*, 4 vols. (Halle, Germany: Waisenhaus, 1700–1702), 1:176.

95 Spener, *Pia Desideria*, 103; Spener, *Theologische Bedencken*, 2:272. See also K. James Stein, *Philipp Jakob Spener: Pietist Patriarch* (Chicago:

Covenant, 1986), 216–18. For his claims that the minister does not affect the power of the word or the office, see Spener, *Pia Desideria*, 46; and Spener, *Theologische Bedencken*, 1:488.

96 Spener, *Theologische Bedencken*, 3:674–75, 688, 1:440. See also 4:387. For his indecision, see Stein, *Philipp Jakob Spener*, 74, 108, 125.

97 Stein, *Philipp Jakob Spener*, 108–9; Chauncey David Ensign, "Radical German Pietism (c. 1675–c. 1760)" (PhD diss., Boston University School of Theology, 1955), 86.

98 Spener, *Theologische Bedencken*, 1:524, 451, 3:851, 701, 1:524, 441.

99 Mary Fulbrook, *Piety and Politics: Religion and the Rise of Absolutism in England, Wurttemberg and Prussia* (Cambridge: Cambridge University Press, 1983), 96–97.

100 Cited in Mary Bernadette Havens, "Zinzendorf and the 'Augsburg Confession': An Ecumenical Vision?" (PhD diss., Princeton Theological Seminary, 1990), 31. See Markus Matthias, "August Herman Francke," in *The Pietist Theologians: An Introduction to Theology in the Seventeenth and Eighteenth Centuries*, ed. Carter Lindberg (Malden, MA: Blackwell, 2005), 107–8.

101 Cited in Gary R. Sattler, *God's Glory, Neighbor's Good: A Brief Introduction to the Life and Writings of August Hermann Francke* (Chicago: Covenant, 1982), 196.

102 August Hermann Francke, "Predigt von Den Falschen Propheten, 1698," in *Werke in Auswahl*, ed. Erhard Peschke (Berlin: Evangelische Verlagsanstalt, 1969), 329; Matthias, "August Herman Francke," 110; Jonathan Strom, "Pietist Experiences and Narratives of Conversion," in *A Companion to German Pietism, 1660–1800*, ed. Douglas Shantz (Leiden: Brill, 2014), 310; Tom Bach, "The Halle Testimonial System: Conflicts and Controversies," *Covenant Quarterly* 64, no. 4 (November 2006): 39–55.

103 Francke, "Predigt," 310.

104 Francke, 311. See Sattler, *God's Glory, Neighbor's Good*, 42–43.

105 Citations in Havens, "Zinzendorf," 207–13, 470, 106, 505–6, 212. See also August Gottlieb Spangenberg, *The Life of Nicholas Lewis Count Zinzendorf*, trans. S. Jackson (London: Samuel Holdsworth, 1838), 182; and Walter H. Wagner, *The Zinzendorf-Muhlenberg Encounter: A Controversy in Search of Understanding* (Nazareth, PA: Moravian Historical Society, 2002), 57.

106 Wagner, Zinzendorf-Muhlenberg Encounter, 56.

107 Havens, "Zinzendorf," 229–30, 425, 440.

108 Cited in Wagner, Zinzendorf-Muhlenberg Encounter, 57.

109 Havens, "Zinzendorf," 343–49.

110 Spangenberg, Nicholas Lewis Count Zinzendorf, 288.

111 Havens, "Zinzendorf," 301, 304.

Chapter 2: American Developments

1 A detailed account is found in Theodore Emanuel Schmauk, A History of the Lutheran Church in Pennsylvania, 1638–1820: From the Original Sources (Philadelphia: General Council, 1903), 493–576.

2 J. Taylor Hamilton, "The Confusion at Tulpehocken," Transactions of the Moravian Historical Society 4, no. 5 (1895): 250.

3 Julius Friedrich Sachse, Justus Falckner, Mystic and Scholar, Devout Pietist in Germany, Hermit on the Wissahickon, Missionary on the Hudson (Philadelphia: printed by the author, 1903), 112.

4 John Ludwig Schulze et al., eds., Hallesche Nacrichten: Reports of the United German Evangelical Lutheran Congregations in North America, Specially in Pennsylvania, trans. C. W. Schaeffer (Reading, PA: Pilger Book Store, 1882), 1:144.

5 Sachse, Justus Falckner, 67 (emphasis added).

6 Simon Hart and Harry J. Kreider, trans., Lutheran Church in New York and New Jersey, 1722–1760: Lutheran Records in the Ministerial Archives of the Staatsarchiv, Hamburg, Germany (New York: United Lutheran Synod of New York and New England, 1962), 3.

7 Schulze et al., Hallesche Nacrichten, 1:141, 143. See also Schulze et al., 1:32–33.

8 Schulze et al., 1:102. See also Leonard R. Riforgiato, Missionary of Moderation: Henry Melchior Muhlenberg and the Lutheran Church in English America (Lewisburg, PA: Bucknell University Press, 1980), 66–70.

9 Riforgiato, Missionary of Moderation, 91. See also Craig D. Atwood, "'The Hallensians Are Pietists; Aren't You a Hallensian?' Muhlenberg's Conflict with the Moravians in America," Journal of Moravian History 12, no. 1 (2012): 60; and Wagner, Zinzendorf-Muhlenberg Encounter, 83. Strohmidel argues, however, that Francke's dispatching

of Muhlenberg was not in direct response to the Moravian threat. Karl Otto Strohmidel, "Henry Melchior Muhlenberg's European Heritage," *Lutheran Quarterly* 6, no. 1 (1992): 5–34.

10 Wagner, *Zinzendorf-Muhlenberg Encounter*, 111.

11 Muhlenberg seemed to echo the early Luther, telling the Hackensack believers in August 1759 that they were "at perfect liberty to beseech God for a faithful pastor and to seek, call, and maintain one without consulting me." Henry Melchior Muhlenberg, *The Journals of Henry Melchior Muhlenberg*, trans. Theodore G. Tappert and John W. Doberstein, 3 vols. (Philadelphia: Evangelical Lutheran Ministerium of Pennsylvania and Adjacent States, 1942–58), 1:408.

12 Riforgiato, *Missionary of Moderation*, 164–66, 176–78.

13 Atwood, "Hallensians Are Pietists," 79–83; Riforgiato, *Missionary of Moderation*, 97–99.

14 Muhlenberg, *Journals*, 1:446.

15 C. W. Schaeffer, "Muhlenberg's Defence of Pietism," *Lutheran Church Review* 12, no. 4 (1893): 357.

16 Schaeffer, 362–63.

17 As Muhlenberg said, "Hirelings may often furnish nothing but straw; and yet there is always some good grains concealed in it." Schaeffer, 358.

18 Muhlenberg, *Journals*, 2:136.

19 Schaeffer, "Muhlenberg's Defence of Pietism," 369.

20 Muhlenberg, *Journals*, 2:137.

21 Schulze et al., *Hallesche Nachrichten*, 1:209–10.

22 Schulze et al., 1:210.

23 Evangelical Lutheran Ministerium of Pennsylvania and the Adjacent States, *Documentary History of the Evangelical Lutheran Ministerium of Pennsylvania and Adjacent States* (Philadelphia: Board of Publication of the General Council of the Evangelical Lutheran Church in North America, 1898), 11.

24 John Wesley, *The Works of the Rev. John Wesley* (New York: J. & J. Harper, 1827), 10:208; Isaac Backus, *All True Ministers of the Gospel Are Called into That Work by the Special Influences of the Holy Spirit* [. . .] (Boston, 1754).

25 Simeon Walcher Harkey, *The Character and Value of an Evangelical Ministry* (Baltimore: T. N. Kurtz, 1853), 13, 14.

26 "A Call to Ministry," *Evangelical Review* 12, no. 46 (1860): 213, 202, 204, 198.

27 Samuel Simon Schmucker, *Elements of Popular Theology, with Special Reference to the Doctrines of the Reformation, as Avowed before, the Diet at Augsburg, in 1530,* 2nd ed. (New York: Leavitt, Lord, 1834), 189–90. For Miller's influence, see James Haney, "The Religious Heritage and Education of Samuel Simon Schmucker: A Study in the Rise of 'American Lutheranism'" (PhD diss., Yale University, 1968), 452–53.

28 H. L. Dox, "A Call to the Christian Ministry," *Evangelical Quarterly Review* 13, no. 51 (1862): 424.

29 "Call to Ministry," 198.

30 S. A. Holman, "The Laborers Are Few," *Evangelical Quarterly Review* 15, no. 64 (1865): 591; Henry Ziegler, *The Pastor: His Relation to Christ and the Church* (Philadelphia: Lutheran Board of Publication, 1876), 17; Jacob A. Clutz, "The Call to the Ministry," *Lutheran Quarterly* 31, no. 3 (1901): 497.

31 In order, quotes are from Ziegler, *Pastor,* 13; Clutz, "Call to the Ministry," 473; G. Diehl, "The Divine and Human Factors in the Call to the Ministerial Office, according to the Older Lutheran Authorities," in *First Lutheran Free Diet in America, Philadelphia, December 27–28, 1877: The Essays, Debates, and Proceedings,* ed. H. E. Jacobs (Philadelphia: J. F. Smith, 1878), 301; and J. R. Dimm, "The Lutheran Estimate of Ordination," in *The First General Conference of Lutherans in America, Held in Philadelphia, December 27–29, 1898: Proceedings, Essays and Debates* (Philadelphia: General Council Publication Board and Lutheran Publication Society, 1899), 328.

32 Schmucker, *Elements of Popular Theology,* 189–90. See also Harkey, *Evangelical Ministry,* 17–18; G. B. Hiller, "The Call to the Ministry," *Luther League Review* 22, no. 6 (June 1909): 18; and R. A. Fink, "Strange Fire Worshipers," *Quarterly Review of the Evangelical Lutheran Church* 1, no. 3 (1871): 361.

33 L. A. Gotwald, "Church Orders: The Necessity of a Right Call to the Office of the Ministry," *Lutheran Quarterly* 9, no. 4 (1879): 526, 530, 531.

34 "Call to Ministry," 197–98.

35 Cited in Clutz, "Call to the Ministry," 497.

36 Charles A. Hay, *Brief Notes on Pastoral Theology* (Gettysburg, PA, 1891), 5.

37 Diehl, "Divine and Human Factors," 300.

38 Charles A. Hay, "The Ministerium," *Evangelical Review* 12, no. 47 (1861): 413–14. See also [Johann Wilhelm Friedrick] Hoefling, "Liturgical Studies," trans. Henry S. Laser, *Evangelical Review* 10, no. 37 (1858): 120–21.

39 Ziegler, *Pastor*, 22.

40 Diehl, "Divine and Human Factors," 300. See also Samuel Schwarm, "The Christian Ministry," *Lutheran Observer*, November 8, 1901, 1410.

41 Harkey, *Evangelical Ministry*, 16–18. The quote is from p. 17.

42 Cited in Raymond Morris Bost, "The Reverend John Bachman and the Development of Southern Lutheranism" (PhD diss., Yale University, 1963), 121. See also Holman, "Laborers Are Few," 591.

43 F. W. Conrad, *The Call to the Ministry: The Prevalent and True Theories Examined* (Gettysburg, PA: J. E. Wible, 1883), 4.

44 Conrad, 6, 32, 35, 45, 11, 12, 33.

45 Conrad, 45, 47–48, 62; Clutz, "Call to the Ministry," 498.

46 H. E. Jacobs, "The Doctrine of Ministry as Taught by the Dogmaticians of the Lutheran Church," *Quarterly Review of the Evangelical Lutheran Church* 4, no. 4 (1874): 576, 574, 579.

47 Jacobs, 579–80.

48 George Hodges, "The Function of the Church in the World Today," *Lutheran Church Review* 38, no. 2 (1919): 159.

49 Revere Franklin Weidner, *The Doctrine of the Ministry: Outline Notes Based on Luthardt and Krauth* (Chicago: Fleming H. Revell, 1907), 111–12. For another testimony to Krauth's endorsement of the inner call, with nearly verbatim language, see Conrad, *Call to the Ministry*, 42–43. Under his "examination questions" for Krauth's "theses on ordination," Weidner includes "discuss the inner call." Weidner, *Doctrine of the Ministry*, 141.

50 C. Armand Miller, "The Office and Work of the Holy Ministry," *Lutheran Church Review* 20, no. 4 (1901): 524–25.

51 George Henry Gerberding, *The Lutheran Pastor* (Philadelphia: Lutheran Publication Society, 1902), 44–45.

52 Jacob Fry, *The Pastor's Guide, or Rules and Notes in Pastoral Theology* (Philadelphia: General Council, 1915), 5.

53 Miller, "Office and Work," 523.

54 C. F. W. Walther, *Church and Ministry: Witness of the Evangelical Lutheran Church on the Question of the Church and the Ministry*, trans. J. T. Mueller (St. Louis: Concordia, 1987), 22.

55 T[heodore] Brohm, "On the Orderly Call to the Office of Preaching," in *C. F. W. Walther's Original Der Lutheraner Year One (1844–45): The Doctrine of the Church*, trans. Joel R. Baseley (Dearborn, MI: Mark V Productions, 2010), 159.

56 "Editorials," *Lutheran Witness*, July 21, 1901, 25.

57 "Literarisches," *Lehre und Wehre* 21, no. 10 (1875): 308–11; "The Reviewer," *Lutheran Witness*, December 4, 1902, 200.

58 "Wandering Evangelists," *Lutheran Witness*, September 7, 1899, 52.

59 C. F. W. Walther, *Americanisch-Lutherische Pastoraltheologie*, 4th ed. (St. Louis: Concordia, 1897), 35. See C. F. W. Walther, *American-Lutheran Pastoral Theology*, ed. David W. Loy, trans. Christian C. Tiews (St. Louis: Concordia, 2017), 46. For Spener, see *Theologische Bedencken*, 4:521.

60 "Sermon at the Installation of Pastor C. G. Stoeckhardt in the Holy Cross Church, St. Louis, Mo.," in C. F. W. Walther, *Selected Sermons*, ed. Aug R. Suelflow, trans. Henry J. Eggold, vol. 2, *Selected Writings of C. F. W. Walther* (St. Louis: Concordia, 1981), 166.

61 *Lutheran Witness*, February 27, 1902, 39.

62 C. C. Morhart, "To Our Boys," *Lutheran Witness* 11, no. 22 (April 22, 1893): 173.

63 Wilhelm Loehe, *The Pastor*, ed. Charles P. Schaum, trans. Wolf Dietrich Knapp and Charles P. Schaum (St. Louis: Concordia, 2015), 6.

64 Matthias Loy, *Essay on the Ministerial Office: An Exposition of the Scriptural Doctrine as Taught in the Ev. Lutheran Church* (Columbus: Schulze & Gassmann, 1870), 114, 124–25.

65 Adolf Hoenecke, *Ev.-Luth. Dogmatik. 4. Mittel zur Aneignung des Heils und Vollendung des Heils* (Milwaukee: Northwestern, 1909), 189.

66 J. Schaller, *Pastorale Praxis in der Ev.-Luth. Freikirche Amerikas* (Milwaukee: Northwestern, 1913), 4.

67 F. A. Johnsson, "Christ and Him Crucified," *Augustana Journal*, October 1, 1896, 2.

68 Conrad E. Lindberg, *Christian Dogmatics and Notes on the History of Dogma*, trans. Conrad Emanuel Hoffsten (Rock Island, IL: Augustana Book Concern, 1922), 470–71.

69 "The Augsburg Confession. Article XIV. Of Ecclesiastical Orders," *Lutheran Companion*, April 21, 1917, 1.

70 *Augustana Journal*, June 15, 1897, 4.

71 "On Catching Men for the Ministry," *Lutheran Companion*, August 31, 1912, 1.

72 Maria Erling, "Molding Ministers to Fit Congregations: Religious Leadership among New England's Swedes," in *Aspects of Augustana and Swedish America: Essays in Honor of Dr. Conrad Bergendoff on His 100th Year*, ed. Raymond Jarvi (Rock Island, IL: Augustana Historical Society, 1995), 192.

73 C. J. Sodergren, "The Crying Demand for Ministers of the Gospel," *Augustana Journal*, November 24, 1906, 3.

74 "Fragments from Our Pastorium and Diary," *Young Lutheran's Companion*, February 9, 1907, 3.

75 Julius Boraas, "Red Wing Seminary: As Julius Boraas Knew It, in 1886–90, 1895–9," n.d., 4, 6, RWS file, St. Olaf College Archives, Northfield, MN; Thomas E. Jacobson, "Hauge's Norwegian Evangelical Lutheran Synod in America and the Continuation of the Haugean Spirit in Twentieth-Century American Lutheranism" (PhD diss., Luther Seminary, 2018), 144.

76 Gracia Grindal, *Thea Rønning: Young Woman on a Mission* (Minneapolis: Lutheran University Press, 2012), 63; Andreas Helland, *Missionary John O. Dyrnes, 1867–1943* (Minneapolis: Lutheran Board of Missions, 1944), 10; *Lutheran Companion*, January 10, 1914, 10.

77 Carroll J. Rockey, *Fishing for Fishers of Men* (Philadelphia: United Lutheran Publication House, 1924), 62, 64.

78 Walton Harlowe Greever, *The Minister and the Ministry* (Philadelphia: Board of Publication of the United Lutheran Church in America, 1945), 6–7.

79 Greever, 7.

80 Wilfried Tappert, "Concerning the Call to the Ministry," *Lutheran Church Quarterly* 16, no. 3 (1943): 277. See also 283. He probably had

in mind "The Call to the Ministry," special committee's report to the United Lutheran Church in America, 1938, 3, ELCA Archives. Tappert's critique did not alter the ULCA's official stance nine years later that "Christ calls men through his Church." See *Minutes of the 18th Biennial Convention of the United Lutheran Church in America* (1952), 551, ELCA Archives.

81 Norwegian Lutheran Church of America, *Official Reports to the Norwegian Lutheran Church of America, for the* [. . .] *Regular District Conventions* (Minneapolis: Augsburg, 1931), 860.

82 Norwegian Lutheran Church of America, *Annual Report, District Conventions* (Minneapolis: Augsburg, 1937), 279. Similar sentiments are in Evangelical Lutheran Church, *Annual Report, District Conventions* (Minneapolis: Augsburg, 1953), 546, 552.

83 ELC report, Minneapolis, June 21–27, 1950, 52, cited in Paul John Kirsch, "Deaconesses in the United States since 1918: A Study of the Deaconess Work of the United Lutheran Church in America in Comparison with the Corresponding Programs of the Other Lutheran Churches and of the Evangelical and Reformed, Mennonite, Episcopal, and Methodist Churches" (PhD diss., New York University, 1961), 323.

84 A. D. Mattson, *Polity of the Augustana Lutheran Church* (Rock Island, IL: Augustana Book Concern, 1952), 76–77.

85 Walter Erwin Schuette, *Keeping the Faith: Sermons for Special Occasions* (Columbus: Wartburg, 1942), 69.

86 John H. C. Fritz, *Pastoral Theology; a Handbook of Scriptural Principles Written Especially for Pastors of the Lutheran Church* (St. Louis: Concordia, 1945), 42.

87 William F. Arndt, "The Doctrine of the Call into the Holy Ministry," *Concordia Theological Monthly* 25, no. 5 (May 1954): 342, 347.

88 William Larson, ed., *Reports and Actions of the Second General Convention of the American Lutheran Church* (Columbus, 1964), 140.

89 Arnold R. Mickelson, ed., *Reports and Actions: Eighth General Convention of the American Lutheran Church* (1976), 1059, 1060.

90 *Minutes: Fifth Biennial Convention of the Lutheran Church in America* (Minneapolis, 1970), 431, ELCA Archives.

91 *The Ministry of the Church: A Lutheran Understanding* (Division of Theological Studies, Lutheran Council in the USA, 1974), 4, ELCA Archives.

92 Walter R. Wietzke and Wayne C. Stumme, "Definition of Ordination," letter to Board for Theological Education and Ministry, American Lutheran Church, March 15, 1982, ELCA Archives.

93 Marjorie Gerhart, *Women in the Ordained Ministry: A Report to the Division for Professional Leadership, Lutheran Church in America* (Philadelphia, 1976), 6–7, 11; Donna L. Koch, "Theology, Tradition, and Turbulent Times: Ordination of Women in the Lutheran Church, 1970" (MA thesis, Old Dominion University, 2001), 159–60; Marcelle Ilona Williams, "Women's Ordination in the United States: A Comparative Study of Women's Struggle in the Roman Catholic Church, Episcopal Church, and Evangelical Lutheran Church in America" (PhD diss., California Institute of Integral Studies, 2016), 103; Jane Strohl, "The Call to Ministry of Word and Sacrament," in *Serving the Word: Lutheran Women Consider Their Calling*, ed. Marilyn Preus (Minneapolis: Augsburg, 1988), 113–22.

94 Paul Raymond Nelson, "Lutheran Ordination in North America: The 1982 Rite" (PhD diss., University of Notre Dame, 1987), 31, 105, 108.

95 Nelson, 109.

96 Quotations from Nelson, 110–11.

97 "Theology and Practice of the Divine Call," Commission on Theology and Church Relations, Lutheran Church–Missouri Synod, 2003, 30, https://files.lcms.org/file/preview/RLmPR2bcQACzFjd4XYpX8 sjBHtakFYKS?. See also p. 34, concerning transferring to a new pastorate. Interestingly, the Lutheran Church–Canada, which is separate from but in close relationship with the Missouri Synod, more forcefully rejected inner call theology, especially in the context of women's ordination. "Theses on the Role of Women in the Church," Commission on Theology and Church Relations, Lutheran Church–Canada, 1996, note 19, https://www.lutheranchurchcanada.ca/wp-content/uploads/sites/11/2019/07/Theses-on-The-Role-of-Women-in-The -Church.pdf.

98 "Visions and Expectations: Ordained Ministers in the Evangelical Lutheran Church in America," ELCA, 1990, 5, https://www.elm .org/wp-content/uploads/2017/07/Vision_and_Expectations_for _Ordained_Ministers.pdf.

99 "Together for Ministry: Final Report and Actions on the Study of Ministry, 1988–1993," ELCA, 1993, 14, http://download.elca.org/ELCA%20Resource%20Repository/Together_for_Ministry.pdf.

100 "Call Process Handbook," 5.

101 "A Guide to the MDS for Bishops, Call Process Administrators, Churchwide Personnel," ELCA, 2015, 4, http://download.elca.org/ELCA%20Resource%20Repository/Guide_to_the_MDS_2017.pdf?_ga=2.215414551.1072540470.1528549594-35237266.1524007880.

102 "Candidacy Manual," ELCA, revised 2021, 5, https://download.elca.org/ELCA%20Resource%20Repository/Candidacy_Manual_2021.pdf?_ga=2.244615939.722996641.1615675825-2089965714.1608165201.

103 Walter R. Bouman and Sue M. Setzer, *What Shall I Say? Discerning God's Call to Ministry* (Chicago: ELCA, 1995), 54, 40, 49, 57.

104 Paul Baglyos, *Called to Lead—God's Call, Your Vocation: A Discernment Guide Regarding Ministry in the Evangelical Lutheran Church in America* (Chicago: ELCA, 2019), 21–22, https://download.elca.org/ELCA%20Resource%20Repository/Called_to_Lead.pdf.

Chapter 3: Calling and Vocations

1 BC, 299 (emphasis added). The German word is "Stände," variously translated as "walks of life," "vocations," "estates," or "callings." The preface was added in 1538.

2 Gustaf Wingren, *Luther on Vocation*, trans. Carl C. Rasmussen (Philadelphia: Muhlenberg, 1957); Mark D. Tranvik, *Martin Luther and the Called Life* (Minneapolis: Fortress, 2016); D. Michael Bennethum, *Listen! God Is Calling! Luther Speaks of Vocation, Faith, and Work* (Minneapolis: Augsburg Fortress, 2003).

3 John Nicholas Lenker, ed., *The Precious and Sacred Writings of Martin Luther* (Minneapolis: Lutherans in All Lands, 1905), 10:34.

4 Wingren, *Luther on Vocation*, 148.

5 Einar Billing, *Our Calling*, trans. Conrad Bergendoff (Philadelphia: Fortress, 1964), 27.

6 Gene Edward Veith Jr., *God at Work: Your Christian Vocation in All of Life* (Wheaton, IL: Crossway, 2011), 49.

7 Edward P. Hahnenberg, *Awakening Vocation: A Theology of Christian Call* (Collegeville, MN: Michael Glazier, 2010), 193.

8 Douglas James Schuurman, *Vocation: Discerning Our Callings in Life* (Grand Rapids, MI: Eerdmans, 2004), 148. Schuurman elsewhere equivocates, "When a Christian perceives a genuine human need and has the abilities needed for attending to it, that need becomes a spark of God's calling to him." Schuurman, 39. What, exactly, is a spark? Is it God's call or not? Writers on vocation always seem to want a pious spiritual distance between the earth and God's living voice, mediated through some human psychological process.

9 Mark D. Tranvik, "The Good Samaritan as Good News: Martin Luther and the Recovery of the Gospel in Preaching," *Word & World* 38, no. 3 (2018): 258–59, citing (with minor alterations) Eugene F. A. Klug, ed., *Sermons of Martin Luther: The House Postils* (Grand Rapids, MI: Baker, 1996), 2:410.

10 Hahnenberg, *Awakening Vocation*, 194.

11 Tranvik, "Good Samaritan," 258, citing Klug, *Sermons of Martin Luther*, 2:420.

12 *LW* 1:103–4, 115.

13 Marc Kolden, "Christian Vocation in Light of Feminist Critiques," *Lutheran Quarterly* 10, no. 1 (1996): 71, citing *LW* 14:114.

14 Marc Kolden, "Luther on Vocation," *Word & World* 3, no. 4 (1983): 386.

15 Oswald Bayer, "Nature and Institution: Luther's Doctrine of the Three Orders," trans. Luis Dreher, *Lutheran Quarterly* 12, no. 2 (1998): 125–26, 134.

16 *LW* 21:37–38.

17 *LW* 21:256.

18 *LW* 21:237, cited in Wingren, *Luther on Vocation*, 72.

19 Schuurman, *Vocation*, 119.

20 Theodore G. Tappert, ed., *Luther: Letters of Spiritual Counsel* (Vancouver, BC: Regent College Publishing, 2003), 233.

21 Parker J. Palmer, *Let Your Life Speak: Listening for the Voice of Vocation* (New York: John Wiley & Sons, 1999), 67, 10. See Schuurman, *Vocation*, 45.

22 Tappert, *Luther*, 236.

23 Bayer, "Nature and Institution," 145, citing *LW* 37:365.

24 *LW* 1:116.

25 Michael J. Berg, "Masks of God: Vocation as the Proper Setting for Human Flourishing" (DMin thesis, Biola University, 2017), 3. See also Billing, *Our Calling*; Tranvik, *Martin Luther*, 70; and Kolden, "Christian Vocation," 77, 81.

26 *LW* 21:269. See also *LW* 21:258.

27 As Wingren wrote, "Apart from relation with God, man has an office, established by God, but not a vocation." Wingren, *Luther on Vocation*, 91. See also Berg, "Masks of God," 3, 75; and Allen Jorgenson, "Crux et Vocatio," *Scottish Journal of Theology* 62, no. 3 (2009): 291. While agreeing with the basic distinction, Veith applies "vocation" to both believers and unbelievers. Veith, *God at Work*, 35.

28 Lenker, *Precious and Sacred Writings*, 10:242.

29 Veith, *God at Work*, 54.

30 Cited in Wingren, *Luther on Vocation*, 212; *WA* 43:210. See also *LW* 24:220; and *LW* 13:370: "Nowhere among men on earth is there a people like the Christians, who understand and teach so well what worldly stations are. They alone know and teach that these are divine ordinances and institutions."

31 Billing, *Our Calling*, 13.

32 Lenker, *Precious and Sacred Writings*, 10:242.

33 Tranvik, *Martin Luther*, 9, 11. See also Schuurman, *Vocation*, 23. The quote is from Schuurman, 46.

34 *The Good Place*, season 3, episode 11, "Chidi Sees the Time-Knife," directed by Jude Weng, aired January 17, 2019, on NBC.

35 Wingren, *Luther on Vocation*, 118.

36 Veith, *God at Work*, 23.

37 See *LW* 21:267: "In other words, you cannot ruin it, since you are living in the divine office and in the Word. Though it might be sin otherwise, it will not be called wrong but will be covered over and forgiven."

38 Steven D. Paulson, *Luther for Armchair Theologians* (Louisville, KY: Westminster John Knox, 2004), 200.

39 Kathryn A. Kleinhans, "The Work of a Christian: Vocation in Lutheran Perspective," *Word & World* 25, no. 4 (2005): 400.

40 Tranvik, *Martin Luther*, 97, citing *LW* 45:40.

41 James Arne Nestingen, "Luther on Marriage, Vocation, and the Cross," *Word & World* 23, no. 1 (2003): 36.

42 Wingren, *Luther on Vocation*, 103, citing WA 18:672.

43 LW 37:365.

44 Wingren, *Luther on Vocation*, 53.

45 Wingren, 88, citing WA 10.1:317; LW 21:244.

46 LW 21:20.

47 Schuurman, *Vocation*, 123. From Lenker, *Precious and Sacred Writings*, 10:37.

48 LW 1:107–8.

49 Hahnenberg, *Awakening Vocation*, 178.

50 Olga Khazan, "'Find Your Passion' Is Awful Advice," *Atlantic*, July 12, 2018, https://www.theatlantic.com/science/archive/2018/07/find-your-passion-is-terrible-advice/564932/. The article cites two studies: Patricia Chen, Phoebe C. Ellsworth, and Norbert Schwarz, "Finding a Fit or Developing It: Implicit Theories about Achieving Passion for Work," *Personality and Social Psychology Bulletin* 41, no. 10 (October 1, 2015): 1411–24; and Paul A. O'Keefe, Carol S. Dweck, and Gregory M. Walton, "Implicit Theories of Interest: Finding Your Passion or Developing It?," *Psychological Science* 29, no. 10 (October 1, 2018): 1653–64. See also Kevin Berger, "This Man Says the Mind Has No Depths," *Nautilus*, July 26, 2018, http://nautil.us/issue/62/systems/this-man-says-the-mind-has-no-depths.

51 Hahnenberg, *Awakening Vocation*, 126.

52 Rachel B. Griffis, "Vocation Is Something That Happens to You: Freedom, Education, and the American Literary Tradition," in *Christian Faith and University Life: Stewards of the Academy*, ed. T. Laine Scales and Jennifer L. Howell (New York: Palgrave Macmillan, 2017), 35.

Chapter 4: Call to the Office of Ministry

1 Molstad, "Pastor's Proper Handling."

2 Hahnenberg, *Awakening Vocation*, 50. Hahnenberg writes elsewhere, "With the spread of infant baptism and the rise of Constantinian Christianity, the language of call became applied less and less to the call to discipleship, and more and more to the call to enter the monastery." Hahnenberg, 10.

3 Hahnenberg, 52.

4 Saint Thomas Aquinas, *An Apology for the Religious Orders: Being a Translation from the Latin of Two of the Minor Works of the Saint* (London: Sands, 1902), 426, 427.

5 "Luther on Galatians," trans. H. R. Hemmeter, *Lutheran Witness* 12, no. 15 (January 7, 1894): 115 (emphasis added).

6 Benjamin T. G. Mayes, "The Useful Applications of Scripture in Lutheran Orthodoxy: An Aid to Contemporary Preaching and Exegesis," *Concordia Theological Quarterly* 83, nos. 1–2 (January 2019): 111–35.

7 Timothy J. Wengert, *Word of Life: Introducing Lutheran Hermeneutics* (Minneapolis: Fortress, 2019), 55, citing *LW* 35:170.

8 *BC*, 582. Evaluating the Scripture-as-means notion is complicated by the fact that its supporters generally refer not to any particular passages of Scripture as conveying this call but rather to a molding of one's dispositions through the words of Scripture in general. This suggests that they are operating with a vastly different framework for applying Scripture than Luther and his early coworkers. Robert Kolb, *Martin Luther and the Enduring Word of God: The Wittenberg School and Its Scripture-Centered Proclamation* (Grand Rapids, MI: Baker Academic, 2016); Wengert, *Word of Life*. Scripture as a tool for molding dispositions has more in common with the Catholic spiritual tradition, as in Ignatius of Loyola's *Spiritual Exercises*, which is intended precisely as an aid to vocational discernment. Hahnenberg, *Awakening Vocation*, 55–56.

9 Steven D. Paulson, "Law and Gospel: Two Preaching Offices," *Dialog* 39, no. 3 (2000): 170. For a fuller discussion of this issue, see Steven D. Paulson, "From Scripture to Dogmatics," *Lutheran Quarterly* 7, no. 2 (1993): 159–69.

10 Gerhard, *On the Ministry*, 181. See also Quenstedt, *Holy Ministry*, 28.

11 Maurer, *Historical Commentary*, 192. For another example, see Harris Kaasa, "The Doctrine of the Church in Norway in the Nineteenth Century" (PhD diss., Durham University, 1960), 19.

12 The Southern Baptist Albert Mohler is the chief culprit and inspiration for other writers who claim Luther insisted on an inner call to ministry, calling it "God's voice heard by faith." Albert Mohler, "Has God Called You? Discerning the Call to Preach," Albert Mohler,

July 19, 2013, https://albertmohler.com/2013/07/19/has-god-called
-you-discerning-the-call-to-preach-2/. See also Tony Merida, *Faithful Preaching* (Nashville: B&H, 2009), 49.

13   Mark A. Cook, "Luther's Pastoral Leadership," in *Luther on Leadership: Leadership Insights from the Great Reformer*, ed. David D. Cook
(Eugene, OR: Wipf & Stock, 2017), 126–27; Spijker, *Ecclesiastical
Offices*, 397. Rupp claims that Karlstadt's stress on the inner call may
have been his response to Luther, who "says little about the inward
call" in his tract "Concerning the Ministry." Gordon Rupp, *Patterns
of Reformation* (Eugene, OR: Wipf & Stock, 2009), 122.

14   LW 40:222–23.

15   LW 40:384. See also LW 40:144–45.

16   LW 40:113.

17   LW 40:191.

18   LW 40:111. Karlstadt possibly was not receiving his full archdea-
con's stipend at this time, making Luther's claim somewhat dubious.
Sider, *Andreas Bodenstein von Karlstadt*, 11:180–81.

19   Wolfhart Pannenberg, "Luther's Contribution to Christian Spirituality," *Dialog* 40, no. 4 (2001): 284–89.

20   From Christopher Jackson et al., vocalists, "Where You Are," lyrics
by Lin Manuel-Miranda, music by Lin Manuel-Miranda and Ope-
taia Foa'i, track 3 on *Moana: Original Motion Picture Soundtrack*, Walt
Disney, 2016.

21   LW 13:331.

22   BC, 220.

23   LW 13:332.

24   Timothy J. Wengert, *Priesthood, Pastors, Bishops: Public Ministry for
the Reformation and Today* (Minneapolis: Fortress, 2008), 8. See also
pp. 32 and 42–43.

25   *The State of Pastors: How Today's Faith Leaders Are Navigating Life and
Leadership in an Age of Complexity* (Ventura, CA: Barna Group and Pepperdine University, 2017), 20, 25–26.

26   *Pastor Protection Research Study* (Nashville: Lifeway Research, n.d.),
http://lifewayresearch.com/wp-content/uploads/2015/08/Pastor
-Protection-Quantitative-Report-Final.pdf.

27   Danielle K. Chen, "Pastoral Identity, Calling, Burnout, and Resilience" (PhD diss., Fuller Theological Seminary, School of Psychology,

2020), 4; C. H. Maslach, W. B. Schaufeli, and M. P. Leiter, "Job Burnout," *Annual Review of Psychology* 52, no. 1 (2001): 397–422.

28 Chen, "Pastoral Identity," 19.

29 For example, Chen uses "sense of call" as a synonym for "inner call." Chen, 9, 21–22. It's not clear, however, that subjects in the study would agree that "sense of calling" is the same as "inner call." See also Harold DeSantis Lewis, "A Phenomenological Study of Religious Pastors at Risk for Burnout" (PsyD diss., University of the Rockies, 2017).

30 Lenker, *Precious and Sacred Writings*, 10:247–48.

31 Tappert, *Luther*, 231–32.

32 LW 45:46.

33 "Together for Ministry," 14.

34 LW 21:7.

35 Lenker, *Sermons of Martin Luther*, 4:253.

36 Elert, *Structure of Lutheranism*, 348.

37 Elert, 354.

38 Richard Wilbur, "Love Calls Us to the Things of This World," in *Collected Poems 1943–2004* (Orlando: Harcourt, 2004), 307. Not only is the focus on the love of one's neighbor a rebuttal of the inner call notion, but it also puts into perspective well-worn debates about whether the ministerial office comes through a hierarchy or through democratic processes. As Roy Harrisville writes, for Luther, "neither hierarchical installation nor democratic choice meant anything, but only an act of love." Harrisville, *Ministry in Crisis*, 54. See also Wengert, *Priesthood, Pastors, Bishops*.

39 LW 13:66, 34:103. See Gerhard, *On the Ministry*, 185.

40 Lenker, *Sermons of Martin Luther*, 3:374.

41 Lenker, 4:253.

42 LW 54:80.

43 Ewald M. Plass, ed., *What Luther Says: An Anthology* (St. Louis: Concordia, 1959), 1:5, citing WA 17.2:452.

44 Klug, *Church and Ministry*, 234, citing LW 34:50.

45 LW 22:480.

46 Klug, *Church and Ministry*, 240, citing LW 15:237.

47 LW 48:394.

48 Wengert, *Priesthood, Pastors, Bishops*, 47.

49 Eric W. Gritsch, "The Function and Structure of Gospelling: An Essay on 'Ministry' according to the Augsburg Confession," *Sixteenth Century Journal* 11, no. 3 (1980): 43. See also Conrad Bergendoff, *The Doctrine of the Church in American Lutheranism* (Philadelphia: Muhlenberg, 1956), 19; Mary Todd, *Authority Vested: A Story of Identity and Change in the Lutheran Church–Missouri Synod* (Grand Rapids, MI: Eerdmans, 2000), 208–9; and Eric W. Gritsch, "Convergence and Conflict in Feminist and Lutheran Theologies," *Dialog* 24, no. 1 (1985): 15. For a rebuttal of the notion that "the Lutheran church lacks a 'doctrine of the ministry,'" see Harrisville, *Ministry in Crisis*, 87.

50 Edgar Magnus Carlson, "Doctrine of the Ministry in the Confessions," *Lutheran Quarterly* 15, no. 2 (May 1963): 118–19.

51 Gerhard O. Forde, "The Ordained Ministry," in Nichol and Kolden, *Called and Ordained*, 119.

52 LW 21:276.

53 Lenker, *Precious and Sacred Writings*, 10:45.

54 Wengert, *Priesthood, Pastors, Bishops*, 29. Preaching, teaching, and administering the sacraments solely constitute the office of ministry, but these functions may, for practical reasons, be delegated to separate officeholders. In other words, not every regularly called minister is necessarily responsible for all functions.

55 "Constitutions, Bylaws, and Continuing Resolutions of the Evangelical Lutheran Church in America," ELCA, 2020, sec. 7.31.02, https://download.elca.org/ELCA%20Resource%20Repository/Constitutions_Bylaws_and_Continuing_Resolutions_of_the_ELCA.pdf.

56 "Supplement to the Diploma of Vocation," New Jersey District, accessed January 24, 2021, https://www.njdistrict.org/uploads/3/9/1/4/39146465/supplement_to_the_diploma_of_vocation.pdf.

57 Forde, "Ordained Ministry," 121.

58 Baglyos, *Called to Lead*, 21.

59 Cited in Heidi Droegemueller, Luther Seminary email to the seminary and alumni community, February 13, 2020; and Heidi Droegemueller, Luther Seminary email to the seminary and alumni community, January 22, 2021.

60 "First Call Form," ELCA, accessed January 26, 2021, https://download.elca.org/ELCA%20Resource%20Repository/ELCA_First_Call_Process_Form.pdf?_ga=2.119776392.164797899.1611709519

-2089965714.1608165201; "Rostered Leader Profile," ELCA, accessed
January 27, 2021, 6, http://download.elca.org/ELCA%20Resource
%20Repository/Sample_Rostered_Leader_Profile.pdf.

61 The anonymous survey was administered February 2–March 22,
2021, using Qualtrics and initially sent by email to sixty-six ELCA
synod staff members representing each synod and thirty-four
LCMS district presidents. The survey may have been forwarded, so
there is no guarantee that each synod or district was limited to one
respondent.

Chapter 5: Priesthood of Believers

1 For this definition of *public*, see Stephen M. Squires, "Absolution
and the Universal Priesthood from Luther to Spener" (ThD diss.,
Boston University School of Theology, 2013), 100.

2 Wengert, *Priesthood, Pastors, Bishops*, chaps. 1–2.

3 Lutheran Church in America, Division for Professional Leadership,
*Ministry in the Lutheran Church in America: Study Reports and Official
Documents* (Philadelphia: Board of Publication, Lutheran Church in
America, 1984), 54.

4 Forde, "Ordained Ministry," 123.

5 Schuurman, *Vocation*, 139.

6 LW 21:209.

7 C. Cyril Eastwood, *The Royal Priesthood of the Faithful: An Investigation of the Doctrine from Biblical Times to the Reformation* (Minneapolis:
Augsburg, 1963).

8 For the full argument, see LW 44:115–217.

9 LW 40:21, 13:330.

10 Herschel H. Hobbs, *You Are Chosen: The Priesthood of All Believers*
(San Francisco: Harper & Row, 1990), 15. The classic statement of
this position is Edgar Young Mullins, *The Axioms of Religion: A New
Interpretation of the Baptist Faith*, ed. C. Douglas Weaver (Macon, GA:
Mercer University Press, 2010).

11 Squires, "Absolution," 130, citing LW 6:128.

12 Baptism and the Lord's Supper might also appear to be neglected functions among nonordained Christians. Regarding baptism, "uncommon"
does not mean "neglected," as modern Western medicine makes the

need for emergency baptism by the laity rare. Regarding the Lord's Supper, Luther made two observations that must factor into any assessment about whether it is "neglected." First, since Scripture does not indicate that the Lord's Supper is necessary for salvation, it does not carry the same urgency that attends baptism, preaching, and absolution. Second, when celebrated scripturally, the Lord's Supper is in fact the epitome of the exercise of the universal priesthood, since in 1 Corinthians 11:26, Paul describes the sacrament in fundamentally communal terms involving all who participate in "proclaim[ing] the Lord's death until he comes." See LW 40:22–23.

13   Dorothea Wendebourg, "The Ministry and Ministries," trans. Alexandra Riebe, *Lutheran Quarterly* 15, no. 2 (2001): 160.

14   Acts 21:8 describes Philip as an "evangelist." Although the Holy Spirit directly leads Philip to the Ethiopian, there is no story of Philip receiving a call, from God directly or through the church, to preach and administer the sacraments.

15   LW 39:310.

16   Quenstedt, *Holy Ministry*, 3, 9.

17   Quenstedt, 8.

18   Franz Pieper, *Christian Dogmatics* (St. Louis: Concordia, 1950), 3:440.

19   LW 22:164; Lenker, *Precious and Sacred Writings*, 10:132–33.

20   BC, 405.

21   LW 45:46.

22   Jane Strohl, "Luther on the Family," *Journal of Lutheran Ethics* 3, no. 6 (2003), https://www.elca.org/JLE/Articles/859.

23   Kathleen C. Leonard et al., "Parent-Child Dynamics and Emerging Adult Religiosity: Attachment, Parental Beliefs, and Faith Support," *Psychology of Religion and Spirituality* 5, no. 1 (February 2013): 5–14.

24   Chad Bird, "Parents: We All Choose Our Child's Religion," 1517 (website), March 17, 2021, https://www.1517.org/articles/parents-we -all-choose-our-childs-religion.

25   Robert Kolb, "Parents Should Explain the Sermon: Nikolaus von Amsdorf on the Role of the Christian Parent," *Lutheran Quarterly* 25, no. 3 (1973): 231–40.

26   Veith, *God at Work*, 86.

27   Wengert, *Priesthood, Pastors, Bishops*, 36, citing WA 49:312.

28 Paulson, *Luther for Armchair Theologians*, 96.

29 *LW* 13:333.

30 *BC*, 319.

31 Squires, "Absolution," 131, citing *LW* 22:523.

32 Christopher B. Brown, "Early Modern Midwives and the Lutheran Doctrine of Vocation," *Journal of Lutheran Ethics* 4, no. 2 (2004), https://www.elca.org/JLE/Articles/783.

33 Squires, "Absolution," 196, citing *WA* 10.3:97.

34 *LW* 13:111.

35 Jeffrey M. Jones, "U.S. Church Membership down Sharply in Past Two Decades," Gallup, April 18, 2019, https://news.gallup.com/poll/248837/church-membership-down-sharply-past-two-decades.aspx.

36 Dwight Zscheile, "Will the ELCA Be Gone in 30 Years?," *Faith+Lead* (blog), September 5, 2019, https://faithlead.luthersem.edu/decline/.

37 *WA* 2:430.

38 *WA* 39.2:176. See also *LW* 39:305.

39 Jean Hopfensperger, "Test of Faith: The Unchurching of America: Fewer Ministers, Heavier Burden," *Star Tribune*, August 19, 2018, https://www.startribune.com/fewer-men-and-women-are-entering-the-seminary/490381681/?refresh=true.

40 *LW* 40:32, 39:312.

41 *LW* 39:307.

42 *LW* 44:137.

43 *LW* 44:217.

44 Lenker, *Sermons of Martin Luther*, 3:379.

45 Lenker, 3:384. See also *LW* 25:447.

46 *LW* 39:308–9.

47 *LW* 40:35–36.

48 Lenker, *Sermons of Martin Luther*, 3:389.

49 *LW* 40:33.

50 Merton P. Strommen et al., *A Study of Generations: Report of a Two-Year Study of 5,000 Lutherans between the Ages of 15–65: Their Beliefs, Values, Attitudes, Behavior* (Minneapolis: Augsburg, 1972), 103, 145.

51 "U.S. Protestants Are Not Defined by Reformation-Era Controversies 500 Years Later," Pew Research Center, August 13, 2017, https://www.pewforum.org/2017/08/31/u-s-protestants-are-not-defined-by-reformation-era-controversies-500-years-later/.

52 BC, 341.
53 LW 40:31–32.
54 LW 30:39.
55 LW 39:308.
56 Wengert, *Priesthood, Pastors, Bishops*, 14.
57 LW 36:116.

Selected Bibliography

Arndt, William F. "The Doctrine of the Call into the Holy Ministry." *Concordia Theological Monthly* 25, no. 5 (May 1954): 337–352.

Atwood, Craig D. "'The Hallensians Are Pietists; Aren't You a Hallensian?' Muhlenberg's Conflict with the Moravians in America." *Journal of Moravian History* 12, no. 1 (2012): 47–92.

Bach, Tom. "The Halle Testimonial System: Conflicts and Controversies." *Covenant Quarterly* 64, no. 4 (November 2006): 39–55.

Backus, Isaac. *All True Ministers of the Gospel Are Called into That Work by the Special Influences of the Holy Spirit* [. . .]. Boston, 1754.

Baglyos, Paul. *Called to Lead—God's Call, Your Vocation: A Discernment Guide Regarding Ministry in the Evangelical Lutheran Church in America.* Chicago: Evangelical Lutheran Church in America, 2019. https://download.elca.org/ELCA%20Resource%20Repository/Called_to_Lead.pdf.

Barna Group, and Pepperdine University. *The State of Pastors: How Today's Faith Leaders Are Navigating Life and Leadership in an Age of Complexity.* Ventura, CA: Barna Group, 2017.

Bayer, Oswald. "Nature and Institution: Luther's Doctrine of the Three Orders." Translated by Luis Dreher. *Lutheran Quarterly* 12, no. 2 (1998): 125–159.

Beach, J. Mark. "The Real Presence of Christ in the Preaching of the Gospel: Luther and Calvin on the Nature of Preaching." *Mid-America Journal of Theology* 10 (1999): 77–134.

Bennethum, D. Michael. *Listen! God Is Calling! Luther Speaks of Vocation, Faith, and Work.* Minneapolis: Augsburg Fortress, 2003.

Berg, Michael J. "Masks of God: Vocation as the Proper Setting for Human Flourishing." DMin thesis, Biola University, 2017.

Bergendoff, Conrad. *The Doctrine of the Church in American Lutheranism.* Philadelphia: Muhlenberg, 1956.

Berger, Kevin. "This Man Says the Mind Has No Depths." Nautilus, July 26, 2018. http://nautil.us/issue/62/systems/this-man-says-the-mind-has-no-depths.

Billing, Einar. *Our Calling.* Translated by Conrad Bergendoff. Philadelphia: Fortress, 1964.

Bird, Chad. "Parents: We All Choose Our Child's Religion." 1517 (website), March 17, 2021. https://www.1517.org/articles/parents-we-all-choose-our-childs-religion.

Boraas, Julius. "Red Wing Seminary: As Julius Boraas Knew It, in 1886–90, 1895–9." n.d. RWS File. St. Olaf College Archives, Northfield, MN.

Bost, Raymond Morris. "The Reverend John Bachman and the Development of Southern Lutheranism." PhD diss., Yale University, 1963.

Bouman, Walter R., and Sue M. Setzer. *What Shall I Say? Discerning God's Call to Ministry.* Chicago: Evangelical Lutheran Church in America, 1995.

Brohm, T[heodore]. "On the Orderly Call to the Office of Preaching." In *C. F. W. Walther's Original Der Lutheraner Year One (1844–45): The Doctrine of the Church*, translated by Joel R. Baseley, 158–162. Dearborn, MI: Mark V Productions, 2010.

Brown, Christopher B. "Early Modern Midwives and the Lutheran Doctrine of Vocation." *Journal of Lutheran Ethics* 4, no. 2 (2004). https://www.elca.org/JLE/Articles/783.

Burnett, Amy Nelson, ed. *The Eucharistic Pamphlets of Andreas Bodenstein von Karlstadt.* Kirksville, MO: Truman State University Press, 2011.

———. *Karlstadt and the Origins of the Eucharistic Controversy: A Study in the Circulation of Ideas.* New York: Oxford University Press, 2011.

Burreson, Kent Brauer. "Ordination Liturgies, the Call Process, and the Office of the Ministry in the Landeskirche of Braunschweig-Wolfenbuttel, 1569–1815." STM thesis, Concordia Seminary, 1994.

"A Call to Ministry." *Evangelical Review* 12, no. 46 (1860): 195–214.

"The Call to the Ministry." Special committee's report to the United Lutheran Church in America, 1938. ELCA Archives.

Calvin, Jean. *Institutes of the Christian Religion*. Edited by John T. McNeill. Translated by Ford Lewis Battles. Vol. 21. Library of Christian Classics. Philadelphia: Westminster, 1960.

Calvin, John. *Commentaries on the Book of the Prophet Jeremiah and the Lamentations*. Edited by John Owen. Vol. 3. Grand Rapids, MI: Christian Classics Ethereal Library, n.d.

Carlson, Edgar Magnus. "Doctrine of the Ministry in the Confessions." *Lutheran Quarterly* 15, no. 2 (May 1963): 118–131.

Chemnitz, Martin. *Loci Theologici*. Translated by Jacob A. O. Preus. St. Louis: Concordia, 1989.

———. *Ministry, Word, and Sacraments: An Enchiridion*. Translated by Luther Poellot. St. Louis: Concordia, 1981.

Chen, Danielle K. "Pastoral Identity, Calling, Burnout, and Resilience." PhD diss., Fuller Theological Seminary, 2020.

Chen, Patricia, Phoebe C. Ellsworth, and Norbert Schwarz. "Finding a Fit or Developing It: Implicit Theories about Achieving Passion for Work." *Personality and Social Psychology Bulletin* 41, no. 10 (October 1, 2015): 1411–1424.

Clutz, Jacob A. "The Call to the Ministry." *Lutheran Quarterly* 31, no. 3 (1901): 454–506.

Commission on Theology and Church Relations, Lutheran Church–Canada. "Theses on the Role of Women in the Church." 1996. https://www .lutheranchurchcanada.ca/wp-content/uploads/sites/11/2019/07/ Theses-on-The-Role-of-Women-in-The-Church.pdf.

Commission on Theology and Church Relations, Lutheran Church–Missouri Synod. "Theology and Practice of the Divine Call." 2003. https://files .lcms.org/file/preview/RLmPR2bcQACzFjd4XYpX8sjBHtakFYKS?.

Conrad, F. W. *The Call to the Ministry: The Prevalent and True Theories Examined*. Gettysburg, PA: J. E. Wible, 1883.

Cook, Mark A. "Luther's Pastoral Leadership." In *Luther on Leadership: Leadership Insights from the Great Reformer*, edited by David D. Cook, 121–135. Eugene, OR: Wipf & Stock, 2017.

Diehl, G. "The Divine and Human Factors in the Call to the Ministerial Office, according to the Older Lutheran Authorities." In *First Lutheran Free Diet in America, Philadelphia, December 27–28, 1877: The Essays, Debates, and Proceedings*, edited by H. E. Jacobs, 292–312. Philadelphia: J. F. Smith, 1878.

Dimm, J. R. "The Lutheran Estimate of Ordination." In *The First General Conference of Lutherans in America, Held in Philadelphia, December 27–29, 1898: Proceedings, Essays and Debates*, 237–250. Philadelphia: General Council Publication Board and Lutheran Publication Society, 1899.

Dox, H. L. "A Call to the Christian Ministry." *Evangelical Quarterly Review* 13, no. 51 (1862): 412–427.

Eastwood, C. Cyril. *The Royal Priesthood of the Faithful: An Investigation of the Doctrine from Biblical Times to the Reformation.* Minneapolis: Augsburg, 1963.

Elert, Werner. *The Structure of Lutheranism.* St. Louis: Concordia, 2003.

Ensign, Chauncey David. "Radical German Pietism (c. 1675–c. 1760)." PhD diss., Boston University, 1955.

Erb, Peter C., ed. *Pietists: Selected Writings.* New York: Paulist, 1983.

Erling, Maria. "Molding Ministers to Fit Congregations: Religious Leadership among New England's Swedes." In *Aspects of Augustana and Swedish America: Essays in Honor of Dr. Conrad Bergendoff on His 100th Year*, edited by Raymond Jarvi, 25–45. Rock Island, IL: Augustana Historical Society, 1995.

Evangelical Lutheran Church. *Annual Report, District Conventions.* Minneapolis: Augsburg, 1953.

Evangelical Lutheran Church in America. "Candidacy Manual." Revised 2021. https://download.elca.org/ELCA%20Resource%20Repository/Candidacy _Manual_2021.pdf?_ga=2.244615939.722996641.1615675825-2089965714 .1608165201.

———. "Constitutions, Bylaws, and Continuing Resolutions of the Evangelical Lutheran Church in America." 2020. https://download.elca.org/ELCA %20Resource%20Repository/Constitutions_Bylaws_and_Continuing _Resolutions_of_the_ELCA.pdf.

———. "First Call Form." Accessed January 26, 2021. https://download.elca .org/ELCA%20Resource%20Repository/ELCA_First_Call_Process _Form.pdf?_ga=2.119776392.164797899.1611709519-2089965714 .1608165201.

———. "A Guide to the MDS for Bishops, Call Process Administrators, Churchwide Personnel." 2015. http://download.elca.org/ELCA%20 Resource%20Repository/Guide_to_the_MDS_2017.pdf?_ga= 2.215414551.1072540470.1528549594-35237266.1524007880.

———. "Rostered Leader Profile." Accessed January 27, 2021. http://download
.elca.org/ELCA%20Resource%20Repository/Sample_Rostered_Leader
_Profile.pdf.

———. "Together for Ministry: Final Report and Actions on the Study of Ministry, 1988–1993." 1993. http://download.elca.org/ELCA%20Resource
%20Repository/Together_for_Ministry.pdf.

———. "Visions and Expectations: Ordained Ministers in the Evangelical
Lutheran Church in America." 1990. https://www.elm.org/wp-content/
uploads/2017/07/Vision_and_Expectations_for_Ordained_Ministers
.pdf.

Evangelical Lutheran Church in America, Northern Texas–Northern Louisiana Mission Area. "The Call Process Handbook." 2012. https://www
.ntnl.org/wp-content/uploads/2015/05/CPHandbookv8.pdf.

Evangelical Lutheran Ministerium of Pennsylvania and the Adjacent States.
*Documentary History of the Evangelical Lutheran Ministerium of Pennsylva-
nia and Adjacent States.* Philadelphia: Board of Publication of the General
Council of the Evangelical Lutheran Church in North America, 1898.

Fecht, Johann. *Instructio Pastoralis.* Rostock, Germany, 1728.

Fink, R. A. "Strange Fire Worshipers." *Quarterly Review of the Evangelical
Lutheran Church* 1, no. 3 (1871): 343–364.

Forde, Gerhard O. "The Ordained Ministry." In *Called and Ordained: Lutheran
Perspectives on the Office of the Ministry,* edited by Todd W. Nichol and
Marc Kolden, 117–136. Minneapolis: Augsburg Fortress, 1990.

Francke, August Hermann. "Predigt von Den Falschen Propheten, 1698." In
Werke in Auswahl, edited by Erhard Peschke, 304–335. Berlin: Evangelische Verlagsanstalt, 1969.

Fritz, John H. C. *Pastoral Theology; a Handbook of Scriptural Principles Written
Especially for Pastors of the Lutheran Church.* St. Louis: Concordia, 1945.

Fry, Jacob. *The Pastor's Guide, or Rules and Notes in Pastoral Theology.* Philadelphia: General Council, 1915.

Fulbrook, Mary. *Piety and Politics: Religion and the Rise of Absolutism in England,
Wurttemberg and Prussia.* Cambridge: Cambridge University Press, 1983.

Furcha, Edward J., ed. *The Essential Carlstadt: Fifteen Tracts.* Classics of the
Radical Reformation 8. Scottdale, PA: Herald, 1995.

Gerberding, George Henry. *Lutheran Pastor.* Philadelphia: Lutheran Publication Society, 1902.

Gerhard, Johann. *On the Ministry I—Theological Commonplaces.* Edited by Benjamin T. G. Mayes. Translated by Richard J. Dinda. St. Louis: Concordia, 2012.

Gerhart, Marjorie. *Women in the Ordained Ministry: A Report to the Division for Professional Leadership, Lutheran Church in America.* Philadelphia, 1976.

Gordon, Bruce. *Calvin.* New Haven, CT: Yale University Press, 2009.

Gotwald, L. A. "Church Orders: The Necessity of a Right Call to the Office of the Ministry." *Lutheran Quarterly* 9, no. 4 (1879): 485–592.

Greever, Walton Harlowe. *The Minister and the Ministry.* Philadelphia: Board of Publication of the United Lutheran Church in America, 1945.

Griffis, Rachel B. "Vocation Is Something That Happens to You: Freedom, Education, and the American Literary Tradition." In *Christian Faith and University Life: Stewards of the Academy,* edited by T. Laine Scales and Jennifer L. Howell, 31–49. New York: Palgrave Macmillan, 2017.

Grindal, Gracia. *Thea Rønning: Young Woman on a Mission.* Minneapolis: Lutheran University Press, 2012.

Gritsch, Eric W. "Convergence and Conflict in Feminist and Lutheran Theologies." *Dialog* 24, no. 1 (1985): 11–18.

———. "The Function and Structure of Gospelling: An Essay on 'Ministry' according to the Augsburg Confession." *Sixteenth Century Journal* 11, no. 3 (1980): 37–46.

Haga, Joar. *Was There a Lutheran Metaphysics? The Interpretation of Communicatio Idiomatum in Early Modern Lutheranism.* Göttingen, Germany: Vandenhoeck & Ruprecht, 2012.

Hahnenberg, Edward P. *Awakening Vocation: A Theology of Christian Call.* Collegeville, MN: Michael Glazier, 2010.

Hamilton, J. Taylor. "The Confusion at Tulpehocken." *Transactions of the Moravian Historical Society* 4, no. 5 (1895): 237–73.

Haney, James. "The Religious Heritage and Education of Samuel Simon Schmucker: A Study in the Rise of 'American Lutheranism.'" PhD diss., Yale University, 1968.

Harkey, Simeon Walcher. *The Character and Value of an Evangelical Ministry.* Baltimore: T. N. Kurtz, 1853.

Harrisville, Roy A. *Ministry in Crisis: Changing Perspectives on Ordination and the Priesthood of All Believers.* Minneapolis: Augsburg, 1987.

Hart, Simon, and Harry J. Kreider, trans. *Lutheran Church in New York and New Jersey, 1722–1760: Lutheran Records in the Ministerial Archives of the Staatsarchiv,*

Hamburg, Germany. New York: United Lutheran Synod of New York and New England, 1962.

Havens, Mary Bernadette. "Zinzendorf and the 'Augsburg Confession': An Ecumenical Vision?" PhD diss., Princeton Theological Seminary, 1990.

Hay, Charles A. "Brief Notes on Pastoral Theology." Gettysburg, PA, 1891.

———. "The Ministerium." *Evangelical Review* 12, no. 47 (1861): 401–429.

Helland, Andreas. *Missionary John O. Dyrnes, 1867–1943.* Minneapolis: Lutheran Board of Missions, 1944.

Hiller, G. B. "The Call to the Ministry." *Luther League Review* 22, no. 6 (June 1909): 17–19.

Hobbs, Herschel H. *You Are Chosen: The Priesthood of All Believers.* San Francisco: Harper & Row, 1990.

Hodges, George. "The Function of the Church in the World Today." *Lutheran Church Review* 38, no. 2 (1919): 151–159.

Hoefling [Johann Wilhelm Friedrick]. "Liturgical Studies." Translated by Henry S. Laser. *Evangelical Review* 10, no. 37 (1858): 105–124.

Hoenecke, Adolf. *Ev.-Luth. Dogmatik. 4. Mittel zur Aneignung des Heils und Vollendung des Heils.* Milwaukee: Northwestern, 1909.

Holman, S. A. "The Laborers Are Few." *Evangelical Quarterly Review* 15, no. 64 (1865): 589–599.

Hopfensperger, Jean. "Test of Faith: The Unchurching of America: Fewer Ministers, Heavier Burden." *Star Tribune,* August 19, 2018. https://www.startribune.com/fewer-men-and-women-are-entering-the-seminary/490381681/?refresh=true.

Hutter, Leonard. *Compend of Lutheran Theology: A Summary of Christian Doctrine, Derived from the Word of God and the Symbolical Books of the Evangelical Lutheran Church.* Translated by Henry Eyster Jacobs and George Frederick Spieker. Philadelphia: Lutheran Book Store, 1868.

Jacobs, H. E. "The Doctrine of Ministry as Taught by the Dogmaticians of the Lutheran Church." *Quarterly Review of the Evangelical Lutheran Church* 4, no. 4 (1874): 557–596.

Jacobson, Thomas E. "Hauge's Norwegian Evangelical Lutheran Synod in America and the Continuation of the Haugean Spirit in Twentieth-Century American Lutheranism." PhD diss., Luther Seminary, 2018.

Johnsson, F. A. "Christ and Him Crucified." *Augustana Journal,* October 1, 1896.

Jones, Jeffrey M. "U.S. Church Membership down Sharply in Past Two Decades." Gallup, April 18, 2019. https://news.gallup.com/poll/248837/church-membership-down-sharply-past-two-decades.aspx.

Jorgenson, Allen. "Crux et Vocatio." *Scottish Journal of Theology* 62, no. 3 (2009): 282–298.

Kaasa, Harris. "The Doctrine of the Church in Norway in the Nineteenth Century." PhD diss., Durham University, 1960.

Kelly, Robert A. "True Repentance and Sorrow: Johann Arndt's Doctrine of Justification." *Consensus* 16, no. 2 (1990): 47–69.

Khazan, Olga. "'Find Your Passion' Is Awful Advice." *Atlantic*, July 12, 2018. https://www.theatlantic.com/science/archive/2018/07/find-your-passion-is-terrible-advice/564932/.

Kirsch, Paul John. "Deaconesses in the United States since 1918: A Study of the Deaconess Work of the United Lutheran Church in America in Comparison with the Corresponding Programs of the Other Lutheran Churches and of the Evangelical and Reformed, Mennonite, Episcopal, and Methodist Churches." PhD diss., New York University, 1961.

Kleinhans, Kathryn A. "The Work of a Christian: Vocation in Lutheran Perspective." *Word & World* 25, no. 4 (2005): 394–402.

Klug, Eugene F. A. *Church and Ministry: The Role of Church, Pastor, and People from Luther to Walther.* St. Louis: Concordia, 1993.

———, ed. *Sermons of Martin Luther: The House Postils.* Vol. 2. Grand Rapids, MI: Baker, 1996.

Koch, Donna L. "Theology, Tradition, and Turbulent Times: Ordination of Women in the Lutheran Church, 1970." MA thesis, Old Dominion University, 2001.

Kolb, Robert. *Martin Luther and the Enduring Word of God: The Wittenberg School and Its Scripture-Centered Proclamation.* Grand Rapids, MI: Baker Academic, 2016.

———. "Parents Should Explain the Sermon: Nikolaus von Amsdorf on the Role of the Christian Parent." *Lutheran Quarterly* 25, no. 3 (1973): 231–240.

Kolb, Robert, and Timothy J. Wengert, eds. *The Book of Concord: The Confessions of the Evangelical Lutheran Church.* Minneapolis: Fortress, 2000.

Kolden, Marc. "Christian Vocation in Light of Feminist Critiques." *Lutheran Quarterly* 10, no. 1 (1996): 71–85.

———. "Luther on Vocation." *Word & World* 3, no. 4 (1983): 382–390.

Larson, William, ed. *Reports and Actions of the Second General Convention of the American Lutheran Church.* Columbus, 1964.

Lenker, John Nicholas, ed. *The Precious and Sacred Writings of Martin Luther.* Vol. 10. Minneapolis: Lutherans in All Lands, 1905.

———, ed. *Sermons of Martin Luther: The Church Postils.* Vols. 3–4. Grand Rapids, MI: Baker, 1995.

Leonard, Kathleen C., Kaye V. Cook, Chris J. Boyatzis, Cynthia Neal Kimball, and Kelly S. Flanagan. "Parent-Child Dynamics and Emerging Adult Religiosity: Attachment, Parental Beliefs, and Faith Support." *Psychology of Religion and Spirituality* 5, no. 1 (February 2013): 5–14.

Lewis, Harold DeSantis. "A Phenomenological Study of Religious Pastors at Risk for Burnout." PsyD diss., University of the Rockies, 2017.

Lifeway Research. "Pastor Protection Research Study." n.d. http://lifewayresearch.com/wp-content/uploads/2015/08/Pastor-Protection-Quantitative-Report-Final.pdf.

Lindberg, Carter. "Conflicting Models of Ministry: Luther, Karlstadt, and Muentzer." *Concordia Theological Quarterly* 41, no. 4 (October 1977): 35–50.

Lindberg, Conrad Emil. *Christian Dogmatics and Notes on the History of Dogma.* Translated by Conrad Emanuel Hoffsten. Rock Island, IL: Augustana Book Concern, 1922.

Loehe, Wilhelm. *The Pastor.* Edited by Charles P. Schaum. Translated by Wolf Dietrich Knapp and Charles P. Schaum. St. Louis: Concordia, 2015.

Loy, Matthias. *Essay on the Ministerial Office: An Exposition of the Scriptural Doctrine as Taught in the Ev. Lutheran Church.* Columbus: Schulze & Gassmann, 1870.

Lund, Eric. *Documents from the History of Lutheranism, 1517–1750.* Minneapolis: Augsburg Fortress, 2002.

Luther, Martin. *D. Martin Luthers Werke.* 121 vols. Weimar: H. Bohlau, 1883–2009.

———. *Luther's Works.* Edited by Jaroslav Pelikan and Helmut T. Lehmann. 55 vols. Philadelphia: Fortress; St. Louis: Concordia, 1955–86.

Lutheran Church in America, Division for Professional Leadership. *Ministry in the Lutheran Church in America: Study Reports and Official Documents.* Philadelphia: Board of Publication, Lutheran Church in America, 1984.

Lutheran Companion. "The Augsburg Confession. Article XIV. Of Ecclesiastical Orders." April 21, 1917.

Lutheran Companion. "On Catching Men for the Ministry." August 31, 1912.

Maslach, C. H., W. B. Schaufeli, and M. P. Leiter. "Job Burnout." *Annual Review of Psychology* 52, no. 1 (2001): 397–422.

Matthias, Markus. "August Herman Francke." In *The Pietist Theologians: An Introduction to Theology in the Seventeenth and Eighteenth Centuries,* edited by Carter Lindberg, 100–114. Malden, MA: Blackwell, 2005.

Mattson, A. D. *Polity of the Augustana Lutheran Church.* Rock Island, IL: Augustana Book Concern, 1952.

Maurer, Wilhelm. *Historical Commentary on the Augsburg Confession.* Translated by H. George Anderson. Philadelphia: Fortress, 1986.

Mayer, Johann Friedrich. *Museum Ministri Ecclesiae.* Leipzig, Germany, 1690.

Mayes, Benjamin T. G. "The Useful Applications of Scripture in Lutheran Orthodoxy: An Aid to Contemporary Preaching and Exegesis." *Concordia Theological Quarterly* 83, nos. 1–2 (January 2019): 111–135.

Merida, Tony. *Faithful Preaching.* Nashville: B&H, 2009.

Mickelson, Arnold R., ed. *Reports and Actions: Eighth General Convention of the American Lutheran Church,* 1976.

Miller, C. Armand. "The Office and Work of the Holy Ministry." *Lutheran Church Review* 20, no. 4 (1901): 523–528.

The Ministry of the Church: A Lutheran Understanding. Division of Theological Studies, Lutheran Council in the USA, 1974. ELCA Archives.

Minutes: Fifth Biennial Convention of the Lutheran Church in America. Minneapolis, 1970. ELCA Archives.

Minutes of the 18th Biennial Convention of the United Lutheran Church in America. 1952. ELCA Archives.

Molstad, John A. "The Pastor's Proper Handling of Call." 2003. http://www .blts.edu/wp-content/uploads/2011/06/JAM-Call.pdf.

Morhart, C. C. "To Our Boys." *Lutheran Witness* 11, no. 22 (April 22, 1893): 173.

Muhlenberg, Henry Melchior. *The Journals of Henry Melchior Muhlenberg.* Translated by Theodore G. Tappert and John W. Doberstein. 3 vols. Philadelphia: Evangelical Lutheran Ministerium of Pennsylvania and Adjacent States, 1942–58.

Mullins, Edgar Young. *The Axioms of Religion: A New Interpretation of the Baptist Faith.* Edited by C. Douglas Weaver. Macon, GA: Mercer University Press, 2010.

Nelson, Paul Raymond. "Lutheran Ordination in North America: The 1982 Rite." PhD diss., University of Notre Dame, 1987.

Nestingen, James Arne. "Luther on Marriage, Vocation, and the Cross." *Word & World* 23, no. 1 (2003): 31–39.

Nichol, Todd W. "Ministry and Oversight in American Lutheranism." In *Called and Ordained: Lutheran Perspectives on the Office of the Ministry*, edited by Todd W. Nichol and Marc Kolden, 93–113. Minneapolis: Fortress, 1990.

Nichol, Todd W., and Marc Kolden, eds. *Called and Ordained: Lutheran Perspectives on the Office of the Ministry.* Minneapolis: Fortress, 1990.

Norwegian Lutheran Church of America. *Annual Report, District Conventions.* Minneapolis: Augsburg, 1937.

———. *Official Reports to the Norwegian Lutheran Church of America, for the* [...] *Regular District Conventions.* Minneapolis: Augsburg, 1931.

O'Keefe, Paul A., Carol S. Dweck, and Gregory M. Walton. "Implicit Theories of Interest: Finding Your Passion or Developing It?" *Psychological Science* 29, no. 10 (October 1, 2018): 1653–1664.

Palmer, Parker J. *Let Your Life Speak: Listening for the Voice of Vocation.* New York: John Wiley & Sons, 1999.

Pannenberg, Wolfhart. "Luther's Contribution to Christian Spirituality." *Dialog* 40, no. 4 (2001): 284–289.

Paulson, Steven D. "From Scripture to Dogmatics." *Lutheran Quarterly* 7, no. 2 (1993): 159–169.

———. "Law and Gospel: Two Preaching Offices." *Dialog* 39, no. 3 (2000): 169–177.

———. *Luther for Armchair Theologians.* Louisville, KY: Westminster John Knox, 2004.

Peter, David J. "A Lutheran Perspective on the Inward Call to the Ministry." *Concordia Journal* 12, no. 4 (July 1986): 121–129.

Pew Research Center. "U.S. Protestants Are Not Defined by Reformation-Era Controversies 500 Years Later." August 13, 2017. https://www.pewforum .org/2017/08/31/u-s-protestants-are-not-defined-by-reformation-era -controversies-500-years-later/.

Pieper, Franz. *Christian Dogmatics.* St. Louis: Concordia, 1950.

Piepkorn, Arthur Carl. "The Sacred Ministry and Holy Ordination in the Symbolical Books of the Lutheran Church." *Concordia Theological Monthly* 40, no. 8 (1969): 552–573.

Plass, Ewald M., ed. *What Luther Says: An Anthology.* Vols. 1–3. St. Louis: Concordia, 1959.

Pragman, James H. *Traditions of Ministry: A History of the Doctrine of the Ministry in Lutheran Theology*. St. Louis: Concordia, 1983.

Puglisi, J. F. *The Process of Admission to Ordained Ministry: A Comparative Study*. Translated by Michael S. Driscoll and Mary Misrahi. 3 vols. Collegeville, MN: Liturgical, 1996.

Quenstedt, Johann Andreas. *The Holy Ministry*. Translated by Luther Poellot. Fort Wayne, IN: Concordia Theological Seminary, 1991.

———. *The Nature and Character of Theology: An Introduction to the Thought of J. A. Quenstedt from Theologia Didactico-Polemica Sive Systema Theologicum*. St. Louis: Concordia, 1986.

Reumann, John Henry Paul. *Ministries Examined: Laity, Clergy, Women, and Bishops in a Time of Change*. Minneapolis: Augsburg, 1987.

Riforgiato, Leonard R. *Missionary of Moderation: Henry Melchior Muhlenberg and the Lutheran Church in English America*. Lewisburg, PA: Bucknell University Press, 1980.

Rockey, Carroll J. *Fishing for Fishers of Men*. Philadelphia: United Lutheran Publication House, 1924.

Rupp, Gordon. *Patterns of Reformation*. Eugene, OR: Wipf & Stock, 2009.

Sachse, Julius Friedrich. *Justus Falckner, Mystic and Scholar, Devout Pietist in Germany, Hermit on the Wissahickon, Missionary on the Hudson*. Philadelphia: printed by the author, 1903.

Sattler, Gary R. *God's Glory, Neighbor's Good: A Brief Introduction to the Life and Writings of August Hermann Francke*. Chicago: Covenant, 1982.

Schaeffer, C. W. "Muhlenberg's Defence of Pietism." *Lutheran Church Review* 12, no. 4 (1893): 349–375.

Schaller, J. *Pastorale Praxis in der Ev.-Luth. Freikirche Amerikas*. Milwaukee: Northwestern, 1913.

Schmauk, Theodore Emanuel. *A History of the Lutheran Church in Pennsylvania, 1638–1820: From the Original Sources*. Philadelphia: General Council, 1903.

Schmeling, Timothy, ed. *Lives and Writings of the Great Fathers of the Lutheran Church*. St. Louis: Concordia, 2016.

Schmid, Heinrich. *The Doctrinal Theology of the Evangelical Lutheran Church: Exhibited, and Verified from the Original Sources*. Translated by Charles A. Hay and Henry Eyster Jacobs. Philadelphia: Lutheran Publication Society, 1876.

Schmucker, Samuel Simon. *Elements of Popular Theology, with Special Reference to the Doctrines of the Reformation, as Avowed before, the Diet at Augsburg, in 1530.* 2nd ed. New York: Leavitt, Lord, 1834.

Schuette, Walter Erwin. *Keeping the Faith: Sermons for Special Occasions.* Columbus: Wartburg, 1942.

Schulze, John Ludwig, J. W. Mann, B. M. Schmucker, and W. Germann, eds. *Hallesche Nacrichten: Reports of the United German Evangelical Lutheran Congregations in North America, Specially in Pennsylvania.* Translated by C. W. Schaeffer. Vol. 1. Reading, PA: Pilger Book Store, 1882.

Schuurman, Douglas James. *Vocation: Discerning Our Callings in Life.* Grand Rapids, MI: Eerdmans, 2004.

Schwarm, Samuel. "The Christian Ministry." *Lutheran Observer*, November 8, 1901.

Sider, Ronald J. *Andreas Bodenstein von Karlstadt: The Development of His Thought, 1517–1525.* Studies in Medieval and Reformation Thought 11. Leiden: Brill, 1974.

Sodergren, C. J. "The Crying Demand for Ministers of the Gospel." *Augustana Journal*, November 24, 1906.

Spangenberg, August Gottlieb. *The Life of Nicholas Lewis Count Zinzendorf.* Translated by S. Jackson. London: Samuel Holdsworth, 1838.

Spener, Philipp Jakob. *Pia Desideria.* Translated by Theodore G. Tappert. Philadelphia: Fortress, 1964.

———. *Theologische Bedencken.* 4 vols. Halle: Waisenhaus, 1700–1702.

Spijker, W. van 't. *The Ecclesiastical Offices in the Thought of Martin Bucer.* Leiden: Brill, 1996.

Squires, Stephen M. "Absolution and the Universal Priesthood from Luther to Spener." ThD diss., Boston University, 2013.

Stein, K. James. *Philipp Jakob Spener: Pietist Patriarch.* Chicago: Covenant, 1986.

Strohl, Jane. "The Call to Ministry of Word and Sacrament." In *Serving the Word: Lutheran Women Consider Their Calling*, edited by Marilyn Preus, 113–122. Minneapolis: Augsburg, 1988.

———. "Luther on the Family." *Journal of Lutheran Ethics* 3, no. 6 (2003). https://www.elca.org/JLE/Articles/859.

Strohmidel, Karl Otto. "Henry Melchior Muhlenberg's European Heritage." *Lutheran Quarterly* 6, no. 1 (1992): 5–34.

Strom, Jonathan. *Orthodoxy and Reform: The Clergy in Seventeenth Century Rostock.* Tubingen, Germany: Mohr Siebeck, 1999.

———. "Pietist Experiences and Narratives of Conversion." In *A Companion to German Pietism, 1660–1800,* edited by Douglas Shantz, 293–318. Leiden: Brill, 2014.

Strommen, Merton P., Milo L. Brekke, Ralph C. Underwager, and Arthur L. Johnson. *A Study of Generations: Report of a Two-Year Study of 5,000 Lutherans between the Ages of 15–65: Their Beliefs, Values, Attitudes, Behavior.* Minneapolis: Augsburg, 1972.

Tappert, Theodore G., ed. *Luther: Letters of Spiritual Counsel.* Vancouver, BC: Regent College Publishing, 2003.

Tappert, Wilfried. "Concerning the Call to the Ministry." *Lutheran Church Quarterly* 16, no. 3 (1943): 275–291.

Tarnow, Paul. *De Sacrosancto Ministerio, Libri Tres.* Rostock, 1624.

Thomas Aquinas, Saint. *An Apology for the Religious Orders: Being a Translation from the Latin of Two of the Minor Works of the Saint.* London: Sands, 1902.

Todd, Mary. *Authority Vested: A Story of Identity and Change in the Lutheran Church–Missouri Synod.* Grand Rapids, MI: Eerdmans, 2000.

Tranvik, Mark D. "The Good Samaritan as Good News: Martin Luther and the Recovery of the Gospel in Preaching." *Word & World* 38, no. 3 (2018): 252–261.

———. *Martin Luther and the Called Life.* Minneapolis: Fortress, 2016.

Van Voorhis, R. Daniel. "A Prophet of Interior Lutheranism: The Correspondence of Johann Arndt." PhD diss., University of St. Andrews, 2008.

Veith, Gene Edward, Jr. *God at Work: Your Christian Vocation in All of Life.* Wheaton, IL: Crossway, 2011.

Wagner, Walter H. *The Zinzendorf-Muhlenberg Encounter: A Controversy in Search of Understanding.* Nazareth, PA: Moravian Historical Society, 2002.

Walther, C. F. W. *Americanisch-Lutherische Pastoraltheologie.* 4th ed. St. Louis: Concordia, 1897.

———. *American-Lutheran Pastoral Theology.* Edited by David W. Loy. Translated by Christian C. Tiews. St. Louis: Concordia, 2017.

———. *Church and Ministry: Witness of the Evangelical Lutheran Church on the Question of the Church and the Ministry.* Translated by J. T. Mueller. St. Louis: Concordia, 1987.

———. *Selected Sermons.* Vol. 2 of *Selected Writings of C. F. W. Walther,* edited by Aug R. Suelflow, translated by Henry J. Eggold. St. Louis: Concordia, 1981.

Weidner, Revere Franklin. *The Doctrine of the Ministry: Outline Notes Based on Luthardt and Krauth.* Chicago: Fleming H. Revell, 1907.

Wendebourg, Dorothea. "The Ministry and Ministries." Translated by Alexandra Riebe. *Lutheran Quarterly* 15, no. 2 (2001): 159–194.

Wengert, Timothy J. *The Augsburg Confession: Renewing Lutheran Faith and Practice.* Minneapolis: Fortress, 2020.

———. *Priesthood, Pastors, Bishops: Public Ministry for the Reformation and Today.* Minneapolis: Fortress, 2008.

———. *Word of Life: Introducing Lutheran Hermeneutics.* Minneapolis: Fortress, 2019.

Wesley, John. *The Works of the Rev. John Wesley.* Vol. 10. New York: J. & J. Harper, 1827.

Wietzke, Walter R., and Wayne C. Stumme. "Definition of Ordination." Letter to Board for Theological Education and Ministry, American Lutheran Church, March 15, 1982. ELCA Archives.

Wilbur, Richard. "Love Calls Us to the Things of This World." In *Collected Poems 1943–2004,* 307–308. Orlando: Harcourt, 2004.

Williams, Marcelle Ilona. "Women's Ordination in the United States: A Comparative Study of Women's Struggle in the Roman Catholic Church, Episcopal Church, and Evangelical Lutheran Church in America." PhD diss., California Institute of Integral Studies, 2016.

Wingren, Gustaf. *Luther on Vocation.* Translated by Carl C. Rasmussen. Philadelphia: Muhlenberg, 1957.

Wohlrabe, John C. "An Historical Analysis of the Doctrine of the Ministry in the Lutheran Church–Missouri Synod until 1962." ThD diss., Concordia Seminary, 1987.

Ziegler, Henry. *The Pastor: His Relation to Christ and the Church.* Philadelphia: Lutheran Board of Publication, 1876.

Zscheile, Dwight. "Will the ELCA Be Gone in 30 Years?" *Faith+Lead* (blog), September 5, 2019. https://faithlead.luthersem.edu/decline/.

Index